CIVIL WAR
GENERALS OF
INDIANA

CIVIL WAR
GENERALS OF
INDIANA

CARL E. KRAMER

THE
History
PRESS

Published by The History Press
Charleston, SC
www.historypress.com

Cover images courtesy of the Library of Congress.

First published 2022

Manufactured in the United States

ISBN 9781467151955

Library of Congress Control Number: 2022943536

Notice: The information in this book is true and complete to the best of our knowledge. It is offered without guarantee on the part of the author or The History Press. The author and The History Press disclaim all liability in connection with the use of this book.

CONTENTS

ACKNOWLEDGEMENTS

This book has been in preparation off and on for more than sixty years, and most people who assisted me are long since deceased and their names forgotten. Those who have passed include my parents, Douglas M. and Jane A. Kramer, who tolerated my collection of Civil War material, much of which I mounted on my brother's and my bedroom walls. Dad and his colleague Mae Smith provided access to library books at the long-gone Speed Community House, where they worked. I also received assistance from the staffs of the New Albany–Floyd County Public Library, the Jeffersonville Township Public Library, the Louisville Free Public Library and the Anderson University Library during the project's early years. My friend Keith Noe, professor emeritus of information technology at Ivy Tech Community College in Sellersburg, Indiana, and my niece, Julia Mensing, provided critical aid with the retrieval and transmission of images. I thank John Rodrigue, acquisitions editor with The History Press, who reached out to me several years ago to see if I had any manuscripts that needed a publisher. I was involved with another book at the time, but when it took a hiatus, I contacted him about this project. He responded affirmatively and has been an ongoing source of support and advice. Mary Kagin Kramer, my partner in both life and business, edited the entire manuscript, catching typographical errors and awkward phrasing while offering love and patience throughout preparation of the final manuscript. Responsibility for other errors of fact or interpretation are mine alone.

.

INTRODUCTION

This book culminates a research project that began in 1961, when I was a freshman in high school. My high school years coincided with the Civil War centennial, which continued into my freshman year at Anderson College (now Anderson University) in Anderson, Indiana. I had a deep interest in American history, and when the centennial began, I began studying the war with great fascination. I haunted libraries and bookstores, created Civil War scrapbooks and began building my professional library. I was especially engrossed in the military side of the conflict, and eventually it converged with an interest in Indiana history that grew from an eighth-grade course on the subject.

As my reading and research proceeded, I focused increasingly on Indiana generals. That curiosity stemmed, in part, from a growing realization that the meaning of "general" varied widely based on context. There were "full-rank" generals, "brevet" generals and "state" generals. There were Regular Army generals and generals of volunteers. There were even "generals" who never held that rank but who were addressed by that honorific by their friends and neighbors. To clarify the confusion, I began researching and preparing sketches of individual generals, all the while attempting to determine their official status. I consulted county histories, Indiana histories, reference books, biographies and other scholarly and popular sources. I was eventually aided by Ezra J. Warner's book *Generals in Blue: Lives of the Union Commanders* (Louisiana State University Press, 1964), which my parents gave me as a birthday gift in 1965. During my research, I made notes on three-by-five-inch cards and placed them in a small green file box.

After graduating from Anderson in 1968, I began graduate work and received a doctorate in American history from the University of Toledo in 1980. During the following decades, I created and operated a historical consulting firm and taught at Indiana University Southeast, including an occasional course in Civil War and Reconstruction. Meanwhile, that little green file box remained on a bookshelf near my business-office desk as a constant reminder of an unfinished task. Finally, in 2020, as the COVID-19 pandemic and other forces slowed consulting activity, I took up the challenge contained in that little green box. The result is a total of 121 sketches, including 44 full Union generals, 1 Confederate general, 62 brevet Union generals and 14 state-service generals.

Under federal policy, full-rank generals were nominated by the president and ratified by the Senate in accordance with their respective Constitutional powers. Brevet appointments, including generalships, were essentially honorary promotions for gallantry or other noteworthy service. State generals were commissioned by governors to militia commands or other positions such as quartermaster, commissary and adjutant generals.

Selection criteria for this volume favored inclusion. The ultimate authority for eligibility of full-rank generals is Warner's *Generals in Blue*, which is derived from various documents related to general officers. The basis for eligibility of brevet generals is a roster of officers of that rank included as an appendix in Warner's book. The authority for state-appointed generals is *Indiana in the War of the Rebellion*, the summary volume of Indiana Adjutant General William H.H. Terrell's multi-volume final report, issued in 1869.

In determining an individual's Indiana connection, I considered three primary criteria. First, anyone born in Indiana is included, irrespective of life tenure in the state. Second, officers born elsewhere but who relocated to Indiana and spent a significant part of their lives in the state are included. This criterion includes some who resided in Indiana before the war and then moved away. Lovell H. Rousseau, for example, was born in Kentucky, moved to Indiana, practiced law and served in the Indiana General Assembly before relocating to Louisville, where he helped organize local defense. Third, persons who arrived in Indiana early in the war, played an important role in organizing the state's military operations and maintained a significant presence after the war are included. As an example, Brevet Brigadier General James Adams Ekin, a Pennsylvania steamboat builder, joined the Quartermaster Corps, arrived in Indiana early in the war and helped Governor Oliver P. Morton organize state quartermaster and construction operations. He remained in the Quartermaster Corps after the war and served as the first commander of the new Western Arsenal in Jeffersonville. There are also a few unique entries. Perhaps most notable, General John Milton Brannan was born and reared in Washington, D.C., but he was admitted to West Point "from Indiana" through the action of Congressman Ratliff Boon and subsequently became a professional soldier.

Collectively, Hoosier generals demonstrated a variety of characteristics that reflect the state of American society. The Civil War was a young man's war, and the same was true for its generals. Of the forty-four full-rank generals, five were under thirty when the war began, and twenty-two were in their thirties. Fifteen were between forty-one and fifty, and just two were over fifty. Brevet generals were even younger, as many moved rapidly through the ranks as officers ahead of them were killed, disabled or given new commands. Twenty-eight of the sixty-two brevet generals were in their twenties and twenty-seven were in their thirties when the war began. Only five were in their forties, and just one was past fifty. Generals in state service were slightly older, with just two in their twenties and only four in their thirties when the war began, while eight were in their forties and fifties. This trend undoubtedly reflected Governor Oliver P. Morton's preference for experienced men, especially in major administrative roles.

Mirroring national migration patterns, Indiana's Civil War generals were a mobile lot. Twenty-one full-rank and twenty-four brevet generals were born in the state, and several moved elsewhere during their lives. But the state attracted even more future generals from other states and some from other nations. Eight full-rank generals were born in Kentucky, while four others arrived from Maryland, District of Columbia, Alabama and North Carolina, respectively, perhaps reflecting the movement of antislavery southern whites to free states. Five others were born in Ohio, and an equivalent number came from New York, Massachusetts and Pennsylvania. The sole immigrant was born in Prussia.

By the mid-nineteenth century, domestic immigration to Indiana was shifting from the southern to the central and northern parts of the state. The nativity of brevet generals, probably because they were younger than their full-rank counterparts, reflected this pattern. The slave states of Kentucky, Tennessee, Virginia, Maryland and North Carolina birthed one each, while adjoining Ohio contributed thirteen and fifteen arrived from New York, Pennsylvania and New England. Reflecting the influx of European immigrants, three brevet generals were born in Germany, and one came from Hungary. Another was born in Canada. The state-service generals hailed from the same states as the full-rank and brevet generals, but the distribution was more balanced. Three each came from Indiana and Kentucky, two were born in Ohio and Virginia and one each migrated from Maryland and Pennsylvania. Two were born in Germany.

Since the war was fought by huge volunteer armies, both the Union and Confederate governments recruited officers from all walks of life, most without military training and experience. Thus, the general officer corps at all three levels was occupationally diverse. Professional soldiers were prized, especially graduates of West Point and other military academies, such as Norwich University in Northfield, Vermont. At least a dozen full-rank generals were professional soldiers, including nine West Point graduates and one Naval Academy alumnus. Several non-academy graduates were Regular Army officers, and many had served in the Mexican-American War. However, there were not enough professional soldiers to command the many regiments recruited for service. So governors relied on community leaders to fill the leadership gap. Because of their high public profiles and political connections, lawyers recruited many regiments and were often commissioned as colonels to lead them. Many became generals as their superiors took new commands or were killed or disabled in action. Other generals included journalists, businessmen, farmers, physicians and a druggist. Indiana-born and Missouri-reared William Anderson Pile was the only minister to serve as a full-rank Union general.

The brevet generals were even more occupationally diverse. Because of their relative youth, the occupations of fifteen brevet generals are unknown. Among those whose occupations are known, more than one-third were lawyers, and only four were professional soldiers, including two West Point graduates. Others included engineers, millers, merchants and numerous business owners, professionals and skilled tradesmen. Lawyers also dominated the state-service general ranks, accounting for eight of the fourteen men who led the Indiana Legion or held administrative positions. The other six included two professional soldiers, a physician, a professor, a building contractor and a merchant.

Regardless of occupation, Indiana generals were politically connected. Fully three-fourths of full-rank generals held some governmental post before, during or after the war. Many were county officials, judges and state legislators, and several were members of the U.S. Congress. About half of all brevet generals held political office, and all but three of the state-service generals held political posts other than their wartime position. Patriotism in the form of a commitment to saving the Union and abolishing slavery was a prime motivation, but so also was a common awareness that defense of the nation might advance one's postwar political career. Posey County politician and judge Alvin Peterson Hovey, for example, was elected governor of Indiana in 1888, and Brevet Brigadier General Benjamin Harrison was elected president of the United States the same year.

Militarily speaking, Indiana's generals were not a distinguished lot. While most served ably and honorably as brigade, division and corps commanders, none succeeded at the highest levels. Major General Don Carlos Buell organized the Army of the Ohio in early 1862 and led it well at Fort Donelson and Fort Henry and at Shiloh. But his failure to follow up after the Battle of Perryville resulted in the loss of his command. Likewise, Major General Ambrose E. Burnside performed well in division and corps commands, but he failed miserably as commander of the Army of the Potomac, ordering successive frontal assaults against entrenched Confederate troops at Fredericksburg, Virginia, in December 1862. At lower levels of command, Brigadier General Mahlon D. Manson's Indiana brigade suffered heavy losses against Braxton Bragg's army at Richmond, Kentucky, in October 1862, and he was captured along with four thousand of his troops. Controversy surrounded Major General Lewis "Lew" Wallace, who got lost and arrived late at the first day of Shiloh. No doubt the most controversial Hoosier was Brigadier General Jefferson C. Davis, who murdered his commanding officer, Major General William "Bull" Nelson, at the Galt House Hotel in Louisville in October 1862. He ultimately avoided courts-martial and served out the war in a series of effective divisional and corps commands, but he never achieved the full rank of major general. Remarkably, in a war in which generals often led from the front, only one Hoosier general died in battle, as Brigadier Pleasant Adams Hackleman sustained a mortal wound while rallying his brigade at Corinth, Mississippi.

This book does not pretend to be the final authority on Hoosier generals in the Civil War. I have attempted to be as comprehensive as possible in identifying those who wore generals' stars for their wartime leadership, but the sketches are necessarily brief. Many subjects, especially brevet generals, lived in relative obscurity before and after the conflict, and documentation about them is thin. Nevertheless, I hope that this work will inspire others to dig more deeply into the lives and tell the little-known stories of the Indiana generals who answered the call to save the Union and end the nation's original sin of slavery.

Full-Rank Generals

Robert Allen

March 15, 1811–August 5, 1886

Robert Allen was born on March 15, 1811, in the village of West Point, Ohio. While the details of his early life are obscure, it is known that he was educated in the local schools. At some point, his family moved to Indiana, from which he was appointed to the U.S. Military Academy at West Point, New York, where he graduated in the class of 1836.

Upon graduation as a second lieutenant, Allen was assigned to the 2nd U.S. Artillery. He served at various posts, including in the Seminole War, until the onset of the Mexican-American War, when he was promoted to captain. He experienced his first combat in 1847 at the Battle of Cerro Gordo, where he was brevetted a major for gallant service. In 1851, he was transferred to the Quartermaster Department, promoted to major and appointed chief quartermaster for the Pacific Department at Benicia, California, where he remained until the Civil War began.

When the war erupted, Allen was reassigned as chief quartermaster of the Department of the Missouri and promoted to colonel in February 1862. He soon earned a reputation for efficiency, which won a promotion to brigadier general of volunteers in May 1862 and responsibility for supply functions in the entire Mississippi Valley. During the following years, operating

Robert Allen. *Courtesy Wikimedia Commons.*

from Louisville, Kentucky, Allen supervised collection and distribution of supplies for major western campaigns, including Grant's Vicksburg campaign and Sherman's Atlanta campaign. He also obtained surplus railroad cars from the Jeffersonville, Madison & Indianapolis yards in Jeffersonville, Indiana, ferried them across the Ohio River and used captured southern rail lines to ship food and other supplies to armies in the field. Before the war ended, his authority expanded to include all supply operations west of the Mississippi except California, and the scope of his responsibility was exceeded only by that of Quartermaster General Montgomery C. Meigs, his West Point classmate.

Allen was mustered out of volunteer service in 1866, having been brevetted a major general, and returned to Regular Army service as a colonel. He retired in 1878 as assistant quartermaster general. During his service, he disbursed about $111 million for equipment and supplies, without a penny being disallowed by the Treasury Department. He died on August 5, 1886, while traveling in Europe and is buried at the Chene-Bougeries Cemetery in Geneva, Switzerland.

WILLIAM PLUMMER BENTON

December 25, 1828–March 14, 1867

William Plummer Benton was born on Christmas Day 1828 in New Market, Frederick County, Maryland. His father died four months later. When Benton was about eight years old, his mother moved the family to Richmond, Indiana, where he gained his early education. During his teens, Benton worked for more than two years as a chairmaker in Cincinnati. The Mexican-American War erupted when Benton was eighteen years old, and he enlisted as a private in a mounted rifle regiment that saw action at Contreras, Churubusco, Chapultepec and Mexico City.

After the war, Benton returned to Indiana and settled in Richmond, where he read law. He was admitted to the bar in 1851 and entered practice with Charles Clark. One year later, he was elected Wayne County district attorney as a Whig. He served until 1854, when he entered a partnership with J.B. Julian. That relationship lasted until 1856, when Benton was elected judge of the common pleas court. He served one term and was defeated for renomination in 1858.

When the Civil War commenced, Benton was one of the first Wayne County men to answer President Abraham Lincoln's call for volunteers. He raised a company and was unanimously elected captain of the 8th Indiana Infantry, a three-month unit, on April 27, 1861. In July, Benton participated in General George McClellan's western Virginia campaign, including the Battle of Rich Mountain. In September, the 8th Indiana reenlisted for three years, and Benton was appointed colonel. The regiment was incorporated with five others into the 1st Brigade, Indiana Volunteers, commanded by Brigadier General Thomas A. Morris. Later in September, the 8th Indiana was sent to Missouri, and in early March, Benton led it at the Battle of Pea Ridge in Arkansas.

Benton was promoted to brigadier general of volunteers on April 28, 1862, and given command of a division in the Army of Southeast Missouri. He led it with distinction during the Battles of Port Gibson, Jackson (where he was slightly wounded), Champion's Hill, Big Black River and the Siege of Vicksburg. During 1864, he held multiple commands with the XIII Corps in Texas and Louisiana, and in early 1865, he led a division in the Mobile campaign. He was mustered out in July 1865 and resumed his law practice in Richmond. In January 1866, President Andrew Johnson nominated Benton for brevet promotion to major general; the Senate approved the award later that month, to rank from March 26, 1865. In 1866, Benton was appointed collector of internal revenue in New Orleans, where he died of yellow fever on March 14, 1867. He was buried at the city's Greenwood Cemetery.

JOHN MILTON BRANNAN

July 1, 1819–December 16, 1892

John Milton Brannan's connection to Indiana was tenuous but significant. He was born on July 1, 1819, and reared in the District of Columbia. During his late teens, he was a messenger in the U.S. House of Representatives, where his performance so impressed Indiana congressman Ratliff Boon that he

John Milton Brannan. *Courtesy Library of Congress.*

circulated a petition among his colleagues to nominate Brannan for admission to the U.S. Military Academy "from Indiana." Upon graduating in 1841, ranking twenty-third in a class of fifty-two, he was assigned to the 1st Artillery Regiment and served at Plattsburgh, New York, during the Canadian border dispute. During the Mexican-American War, as regimental adjutant of the 1st Artillery, he fought at Vera Cruz, Cerro Gordo and La Hoya and was brevetted a captain for gallantry at Contreras and Churubusco. He was severely wounded at Mexico City.

Brannan's Civil War service began on September 28, 1861, when he was appointed brigadier general of volunteers and assigned to command the Department of Key West, Florida. His first combat came in October 1862 at Saint John's Bluff, when he led infantry against Confederate positions for control of Jacksonville. Later that month, he received command of the Department of the South and was brevetted a lieutenant colonel in the Regular Army for his performance at Jacksonville.

In January 1863, he took command of an infantry division in the Army of the Cumberland under General William S. Rosecrans and participated in the Tullahoma campaign, where he fought at Hoover's Gap. In September, he led his division at Chickamauga, under General George H. Thomas, losing 38 percent of his troops in a valiant but ultimately vain effort to hold Horseshoe Ridge. Brannan's stubborn defense won high notice and brevet promotion to colonel and full rank of major in the Regular Army. After U.S. Grant relieved Rosecrans as commander of the Army of the Cumberland, he reassigned Brannan as chief of artillery, a position he held through June 1865. In that post, he oversaw the defense of Chattanooga; fought at Missionary Ridge; participated through the Atlanta campaign, including the Battles of Resaca, Dallas and Kennesaw Mountain; and was present at the siege and surrender of Atlanta. His service won appointment as brevet major general of volunteers and in the Regular Army.

Brannan held several commands in Georgia between July 1865 and May 1866. He subsequently was mustered out of volunteer forces, resumed his Regular Army rank of major and was assigned to the 1st U.S. Artillery regiment. During the next decade, he performed artillery duties at Fort

Trumbull, Connecticut, and Forts Wadsworth and Ogdenburg, New York. While at Ogdenburg, he participated in operations to block Fenian raids into Canada. In 1877, he helped put down riots during the national railroad strike. The same year, he transferred to the 4th U.S. Artillery and served until April 1882, when he retired with the rank of colonel and moved to New York City. He died there on December 16, 1892, and was buried at Woodlawn Cemetery. He later was interred at the West Point Cemetery.

DON CARLOS BUELL

March 23, 1818–November 19, 1898

Descended from seventeenth-century Welsh immigrants to Connecticut, Don Carlos Buell was born on March 23, 1818, in what is now Lowell, Ohio. He lived most of his childhood with an uncle in Lawrenceburg, Indiana, from where he was appointed to West Point. He ranked thirty-second in the celebrated fifty-two-member class of 1841, which produced twenty Civil War generals. After graduation, he served with the 3rd Infantry Regiment in the Seminole War and on frontier garrison duty. During the Mexican-American War, he suffered a severe wound at Churubusco and won brevets to captain and major. He was posted to the Army Adjutant General's office after the war

Don Carlos Buell. *Courtesy Library of Congress.*

and served an extended period in California, rising to captain in 1851 and to lieutenant colonel by the beginning of the Civil War.

Ambitious and well connected in high places, Buell expected that his courage and logistical talent would bring him an important command. On May 17, 1861, while still in California, he was promoted to brigadier general of volunteers. Shortly thereafter, he returned to the East and was charged with organizing the defense of Washington, D.C. Buell's ambitions were blunted when General George McClellan received command of Union forces after the Union defeat at Bull Run. However, McClellan appointed Buell to help organize the Army of the Potomac and then selected him in November to command the newly created Army of the Ohio.

McClellan urged Buell to lead his army into East Tennessee via Louisville and Knoxville, but because of inadequate road and rail facilities, Buell chose to advance by way of the Cumberland and Tennessee Rivers toward Nashville. McClellan and President Lincoln had reservations about the plan, but Buell pursued it with only slight revisions. As it turned out, Buell's plan might have contributed to U.S. Grant's February victories at Forts Henry and Donelson, thus enabling Buell to march into Nashville largely unopposed. His performance earned him a promotion to major general of volunteers in March. In early April, his arrival at Shiloh helped slow the Confederate advance and again contributed to a Grant victory. During the following months, Buell engaged in multiple operations against Confederate forces in the West, including at Corinth, Mississippi, and Chattanooga. But his movements were sluggish, prompting criticism from his superiors and the public.

In September 1862, he advanced into Kentucky to repel the invasion by Generals Braxton Bragg and Edmund Kirby Smith. On September 30, he learned that he was to be replaced by General George H. Thomas. But Thomas argued that Buell was ready to attack and should be allowed to continue. Thomas prevailed, and on October 8, Buell attacked Bragg at Perryville. The battle, though bloody, was indecisive. Bragg withdrew from Kentucky, but Buell failed to follow up, resulting in his removal on October 24. A military committee investigated charges of dilatory tactics but recommended no action. Nevertheless, Buell did not receive another command. He was mustered out of volunteer service in May 1864 and resigned his Regular Army commission on June 1. He soon entered a civilian career, operating an ironworks and coal mine in western Kentucky. During the late 1880s, he served as a government pension agent. He died on November 19, 1898, at his home near Paradise, Kentucky, and is buried at Bellefontaine Cemetery in St. Louis.

AMBROSE EVERETT BURNSIDE

May 23, 1824–September 13, 1881

A native Hoosier, Ambrose Everett Burnside was born on May 23, 1824, in Liberty in Union County. His father was a native of South Carolina and slave owner who had freed his slaves when he moved to Indiana. Educated in local schools, Burnside took up the tailor's trade. But when he was eighteen, his father's political connections enabled Burnside to receive an appointment to West Point. He graduated in 1847, ranking eighteenth in a class of thirty-eight. Posted to the 2nd Artillery Regiment, he performed garrison duty in Mexico City before moving to the southwestern frontier, where he was wounded during a skirmish with Apaches in 1849.

Burnside resigned in 1853 and settled in Bristol, Rhode Island, where he established an arms firm that manufactured a breech-loading rifle he had invented in the army. His company failed, but his personality won him a

Ambrose Everett Burnside.
Courtesy Library of Congress.

commission as major general in the militia and a position with the Illinois Central Railroad, under his friend and chief engineer George McClellan.

When the Civil War began, Burnside organized the 1st Rhode Island Infantry, a three-month regiment that was among the first to reach Washington, D.C. He commanded a brigade at First Bull Run and was appointed a brigadier general of volunteers in August 1861. In early 1862, he commanded a successful expedition against Confederate installations on the North Carolina coast, which won him promotion to major general. During Robert E. Lee's Maryland campaign in September, McClellan assigned Burnside to command his own IX Corps and Joseph Hooker's I Corps to attack Confederates defending a weak position on Antietam Creek at Sharpsburg. Because of poor reconnaissance, he missed several fording points and insisted on bridging the creek, which delayed his arrival at the field and exposed his troops to heavy fire. His units eventually forded the creek about a mile below the bridge, but it was too late to crush the Confederates on the other side.

Despite his stubbornness at "Burnside Bridge," he still had a reputation as an able subordinate. However, he doubted his ability as a senior commander and had twice declined higher command. But in November, after McClellan failed to pursue his advantage at Antietam, Lincoln gave Burnside command of the Army of the Potomac. Recognizing the need to exploit what McClellan had squandered, Burnside determined to attack Lee at Fredericksburg, Virginia, in December. But again, he displayed a combination of stubbornness and irresolution, ordering a succession of fruitless frontal assaults against the impregnable Confederate position on Marye's Heights that cost his army some thirteen thousand casualties—and Burnside his job.

During the next two years, Burnside acquitted himself well in a series of lower commands. As commander of the Department of the Ohio in 1863, he presided over the arrest and sedition trial of former Ohio congressman Clement L. Vallandigham, captured John Hunt Morgan and some of his troops and defended Knoxville against an attack by James Longstreet. In the spring of 1864, he led IX Corps at the Wilderness, Spotsylvania and other battles before winding up at the Siege of Petersburg. Burnside's military career ended abruptly when his troops failed to exploit a huge gap in the Rebel position created by the explosion of a Federal mine in the Battle of the Crater. He was relieved of command and resigned his commission in April 1865. He returned to Rhode Island, served in several business directorships and was thrice elected governor. He was elected U.S. senator in 1874 and served until his death on September 13, 1881. He was buried at Swan Point Cemetery in Providence, Rhode Island.

Robert Alexander Cameron

February 22, 1828–March 15, 1894

Robert Alexander Cameron was born on February 22, 1828, in Brooklyn, New York. In 1843, his parents moved to Valparaiso, Porter County, Indiana. After education in the local public schools, he attended the Indiana Medical College in La Porte, graduated in 1849 and then studied at Rush Medical College in Chicago. By the time he completed his medical education, he had apparently lost interest in medicine and moved into journalism and politics. In 1857, he bought the *Valparaiso Republican* and edited it for several years. In 1860, he was a Lincoln delegate at the Republican National Convention in Chicago and won election to the Indiana House of Representatives.

When the Civil War erupted, Cameron left his seat in the legislature and entered the Union army as captain of the 9th Indiana Infantry Regiment, a three-month unit that participated in George McClellan's western Virginia campaign. When the three-month enlistment expired, he reenlisted and was appointed lieutenant colonel of the 19th Indiana Infantry and then as lieutenant colonel and colonel of the 34th Indiana. With these regiments, he saw service under Major General John Pope at New Madrid, Missouri, and Island No. 10. In August 1863, after the occupation of Memphis, Tennessee, and trench duty at the Siege of Vicksburg, he was promoted to brigadier general of volunteers. Following several stints as a brigade commander in late 1863 and early 1864, he commanded a division in XIII Corps during General Nathaniel P. Banks's Red River campaign in Louisiana. At the Battle of Mansfield on April 8, Cameron's troops attempted to reinforce a failing Union line, but they were pushed back and finally gave way. With the end of the campaign, Cameron served in district command with the Department of the Gulf at Thibodaux, Louisiana. He was brevetted major general in March 1865.

After the war, Cameron pursued interests in town development and farm colonization in Colorado. During the early 1870s, he was instrumental in founding Greeley and Colorado Springs. He subsequently lived for several years in San Francisco and then returned to Colorado, where he served as a postal clerk in Denver and then as warden of the state prison at Canon City, where he lived on a nearby farm. He died there on March 15, 1894, and was buried on his farm.

EDWARD RICHARD SPRIGG CANBY

November 9, 1817–April 11, 1873

Edward Richard Sprigg Canby was a native of Piatt's Landing, Boone County, Kentucky, where he was born on November 9, 1817. After attending public schools in nearby East Bend, Canby moved to Crawfordsville, Indiana, where his father, a former member of the Indiana General Assembly, owned property. He attended Wabash College before securing an appointment to West Point, where he ranked thirtieth among the thirty-nine graduates in the class of 1839. Between graduation and the Mexican-American War, Canby served in the Seminole War in Florida; participated in the removal of the Creeks, Cherokees and Choctaws to Arkansas; and performed various garrison and recruiting duties.

When the war with Mexico erupted, he became chief of staff of a brigade and won brevets to major and lieutenant colonel for gallantry in action. After the war, he held administrative posts in New York and in the adjutant general's office in California during the territory's transition to statehood.

Edward R.S. Canby. *Courtesy Library of Congress.*

Over his objections, the latter job included a year as custodian of the California Archives, usually a civilian post. The archives housed records of California's Spanish and Mexican heritage, and Canby apparently had Spanish language skills that were useful as the government attempted to untangle complex land titles. From California, Canby moved to the Utah Territory, where he served during the Mormon War of 1857–58.

After service in Utah, Canby moved to the New Mexico Territory, where he led the campaign against the Navajos. He was still there, commanding Fort Defiance, when the Civil War began. He was promoted to colonel of the 19th U.S. Infantry in May and given command of the Department of New Mexico in June. In February 1862, he was defeated at Valverde by Confederates under his former subordinate, General Henry H. Sibley, but he subsequently forced Sibley to retreat into Texas following victory at the Battle of Glorieta Pass.

In May 1862, Canby was appointed brigadier general of volunteers and ordered to the East. For the next year and a half, he exercised staff duties, except for command of troops in New York City after the 1863 draft riots. In May 1864, he was promoted to major general and given command of the Military Division of West Mississippi, which reached from Missouri to the Gulf Coast and from Texas to Florida. In that post, he reorganized the troops involved in General Nathaniel P. Banks's failed Red River campaign and joined Admiral David G. Farragut to capture Mobile, Alabama. He accepted the surrender of Confederate generals Edmund Kirby Smith and Richard Taylor on May 26, 1865.

Canby was promoted to brigadier general in the Regular Army after the war, and for the next five years, he did Reconstruction duty in the South and Washington, D.C. He took command of the Department of Columbia in 1870 and the Division of the Pacific in 1873. On April 11, 1873, while negotiating with Modoc Indians for their removal from the Lava Beds in Siskiyou County, California, he was murdered by Captain Jack and others with whom he was dealing. His body was returned to Indianapolis, where he was buried at Crown Hill Cemetery.

ROBERT FRANCIS CATTERSON

March 22, 1835–March 30, 1914

A native Hoosier with an Irish immigrant father, Robert Francis Catterson was born on March 22, 1835, on his family's farm near Beech Grove in Marion County, Indiana. His father died when he was five. After an education at local schools, he attended Adrian College in Michigan and then studied medicine at Cincinnati Medical College. He had recently entered practice in Rockville, Parke County, Indiana, when the Civil War erupted. He volunteered immediately and was mustered into Company A of the 14th Indiana Infantry on April 23, 1861. He advanced rapidly, being successively promoted to first sergeant in early June, second lieutenant later the same month, first lieutenant in March 1862 and captain two months later.

Catterson experienced his first combat at the First Battle of Kernstown on March 23, 1862, when Union troops under General Nathaniel P. Banks encountered Confederates commanded by Major General Thomas J. "Stonewall" Jackson at the opening of the latter's Shenandoah Valley campaign. Catterson's performance was noted by regimental commander Colonel Nathan Kimball, and he was promoted to captain on May 4. Catterson's next action occurred on September 17 at Antietam, where he was wounded. After recovering, he was promoted to lieutenant colonel and given command of the 97th Indiana Infantry in October; six weeks later, he was promoted to colonel.

In 1863, Catterson led the 97th in a succession of major engagements, including the Battle of Memphis on June 6 and its subsequent occupation; the Siege of Vicksburg; the Battle of Tullahoma later in the summer; and the Battle of Chattanooga on November 23–25. During 1864 and through the end of the war, he engaged in Major General William T. Sherman's Atlanta campaign, the March to the Sea and the Carolinas campaign. On November 22, 1864, he was given command of a brigade in Major General John A. Logan's XV Corps. During the Carolinas campaign, he served briefly as Logan's chief of staff and then

Robert Francis Catterson.
Courtesy Library of Congress.

returned to his brigade, which he led until the surrender of Confederate general Joseph E. Johnston at Bentonville. He subsequently was promoted to brigadier general of volunteers, to rank from May 31, 1865.

Instead of returning to medical practice, Catterson relocated to Arkansas in the parade of former Union officers who sought to make their mark in the South. He speculated unsuccessfully in cotton, commanded an African American militia unit used by Governor Powell Clayton to fight the Ku Klux Klan, served as a U.S. marshal and was mayor of Little Rock from 1872 to 1874. When Reconstruction ended, he moved to Minneapolis, where he tried his hand unsuccessfully in farming and selling farm implements. Incapacitated by a stroke, he died on March 30, 1914, in the Veterans Hospital in San Antonio, where he was buried at the national cemetery.

GEORGE HENRY CHAPMAN

November 22, 1832–June 16, 1882

George Henry Chapman was born on November 22, 1832, in the village of Holland, Massachusetts. When he was six, his parents moved to Terre Haute, Indiana, where his father and uncle published a newspaper. After three years in Terre Haute, the family moved to Indianapolis, where the brothers published the *Indiana State Sentinel*. George attended Marion County Seminary and was appointed a navy midshipman in 1847. He served for three years on the USS *Cumberland* and the USS *Constitution* before resigning in 1850 after his uncle's death. Following a brief stint in the mercantile business, he followed his father and uncle into journalism, editing and publishing *Chapman's Chanticleer* from 1853 to 1854 and the *Indiana Republican* from 1854 to 1855. Meanwhile, he studied law and was admitted to the bar in 1857. An ardent Republican, he was appointed assistant clerk of the Indiana House of Representatives the same year and to a similar post with the U.S. House of Representatives in 1859.

Chapman was still in Washington when the Civil War broke out, but he resigned his post in October 1861 and returned to Indiana to serve as a major in the 3rd Indiana Cavalry. After briefly leading the cavalry division of the Army of the Ohio during the spring of 1862, he transferred to the infantry and was given command of a brigade in the Army of the Potomac. During the fall and winter, he fought at Second Bull Run, Antietam and

George Henry Chapman.
Courtesy Wikimedia Commons.

Fredericksburg, earning praise from his superiors and promotion to lieutenant colonel in October 1862 and colonel in March 1863. The following May, he fought at Chancellorsville.

Weeks later, Chapman returned to the cavalry and led a regiment in William Gamble's brigade in John Buford's division, which were the first troops to resist Confederates on the Cashtown road into Gettysburg. Shortly after the battle, Chapman received command of a cavalry brigade in the Army of the Potomac. Between May and October 1864, he led the brigade against Confederate general Jubal Early's forces in the Shenandoah Valley campaign, meanwhile being promoted to brigadier general of volunteers in July 1864 and wounded at Winchester.

In January 1865, Chapman took command of a cavalry division in the Army of the Shenandoah. After the Battle of Waynesboro, Virginia, on March 2, he was ordered to remain in the Valley with only three small regiments and a few artillery pieces, while the rest of the army deployed to Petersburg. On April 19, he was given command of cavalry assigned to Washington. During the months after the war, he served on numerous courts-martial boards. In honor of his service at Winchester, President Johnson nominated him for promotion to brevet major general of volunteers at the time of his resignation in January 1866.

After resigning, he returned to Indianapolis for a judgeship on the Marion County Criminal Court. During the 1870s, he was a bankruptcy receiver for the Louisville, New Albany & Chicago (Monon) and Lafayette, Muncie & Bloomington Railroads. He was elected to the Indiana State Senate in 1880 but died on June 16, 1882, before his term ended. He was buried at Crown Hill Cemetery.

THOMAS TURPIN CRITTENDEN

October 16, 1825–September 5, 1905

A Hoosier by adoption, Thomas Turpin Crittenden was born on October 16, 1825, in Huntsville, Alabama. His father was a younger brother of

U.S. Senator John J. Crittenden of Kentucky, making him a first cousin of Major General Thomas L. Crittenden, USA, and General George B. Crittenden, CSA. Soon after his birth, his parents relocated to Texas, where his father died; soon thereafter, his mother moved to Galveston. Crittenden graduated from Transylvania University in Lexington, Kentucky, where he studied law. He moved to Hannibal, Missouri, where he was admitted to the bar and commenced practice. When the Mexican-American War began, he served as a second lieutenant of a Missouri volunteer battalion for more than a year.

After the war, he moved to Madison, Indiana, where he opened a law practice and married Elizabeth Lorena Baldwin of neighboring Clark County in 1853. When the Civil War began, he entered service on April 19, 1861, as captain of the 6th Indiana Infantry, a three-month unit raised in Madison, and was appointed colonel eight days later. The regiment reenlisted for three years in September and participated in George McClellan's western Virginia campaign. The regiment was reorganized soon thereafter and stationed in Kentucky until the Battle of Shiloh in April 1862, where it was engaged on the second day.

On April 28, 1862, Crittenden was promoted to brigadier general of volunteers, and on July 12, he was posted to command at Murfreesboro, Tennessee. The following day, Crittenden and his entire force were surprised and captured by Confederates under General Nathan B. Forrest. Although Crittenden had not yet had time to become familiar with the town and its force protection needs, General Don Carlos Buell, his commanding officer, scathingly criticized the event as a "disgraceful example of neglect of duty." In any case, the incident virtually guaranteed an end to Crittenden's military career, and he saw no further meaningful service between his release in October and his resignation in May 1863.

In 1868, Crittenden moved his practice from Madison to Washington, D.C., where he remained until 1885, when he retired and moved to San Diego, California, and engaged in real estate development. He died on September 5, 1905, during a vacation trip in East Gloucester, Massachusetts, and was buried with full military honors at Arlington National Cemetery.

MARCELLUS MONROE CROCKER

February 6, 1830–August 26, 1865

Marcellus Monroe Crocker was born on February 6, 1830, in Franklin, Johnson County, Indiana. Although the details of Crocker's childhood and youth are obscure, he entered West Point with the class of 1851 but left in February 1849 to study law. Upon admission to the bar, he began practice in Des Moines, Iowa. With the start of the Civil War, he volunteered for service, was mustered into the army as a captain of the 2nd Iowa Infantry on May 27, 1861, and promoted to major on May 31. In the following months, the regiment was occupied mainly with railroad guard duty in Missouri, during which Crocker's performance earned promotion to lieutenant colonel in September.

Soon thereafter, Crocker was promoted to colonel and appointed to command the 13th Iowa Infantry Regiment, recently organized in Davenport. The unit's first engagement was at Shiloh, where it was part of the 1st Brigade of General John McClernand's division and suffered 172 casualties. A short time later, Crocker received command of the "Iowa Brigade" in the 6th Division, Army of the Tennessee. In that capacity, he fought at Corinth in October 1862, where his performance so impressed his superiors that he was promoted to brigadier general of volunteers the following month. He continued to demonstrate stellar leadership during 1863, when he commanded a division of James B. McPherson's XVII Corps at Vicksburg and conducted a minor raid into Louisiana in September.

The direction of Crocker's military fortunes changed significantly in the spring of 1864. He had suffered for some time from tuberculosis, and in May, while he was en route with the XVII Corps to join Sherman's army in Georgia, he was relieved of command and transferred to New Mexico, where superiors thought his health would benefit from the drier climate. His condition improved from the change, and in December, he was ordered to report to General George H. Thomas at Nashville, Tennessee. But for reasons that are unclear, the order was either miscommunicated or countermanded, and in March, he was transferred to Washington, D.C. Presumably because of the capital's terrible climate, Crocker's condition gradually worsened, leading to his death on August 26, 1865. His body was returned to Des Moines, where he was buried at Woodland Cemetery. General U.S. Grant said of Crocker, "I have never seen but three or four division commanders his equal."

CHARLES CRUFT

January 12, 1826–March 23, 1883

Charles Cruft

Charles Cruft. *Courtesy Wikimedia Commons.*

Charles Cruft was a native of Terre Haute, Vigo County, Indiana, where he was born on January 12, 1826. He studied at Wabash College in Crawfordsville, and after graduating in 1842, he served as a schoolteacher, clerked at a bank and studied law. He was admitted to the bar in 1848 and opened practice with John Baird in Terre Haute. During the 1850s, he entered the railroad business, heading the St. Louis, Alton & Terre Haute Railroad from 1855 to 1858.

Cruft was in Washington, D.C., when the Civil War began, and he was a spectator at the First Battle of Bull Run. He volunteered for service after returning to Terre Haute, and on September 20, he was mustered in as colonel of the 31st Indiana Infantry. His regiment was assigned to a brigade in General Lewis Wallace's division, and in February 1862, he commanded the brigade at General U.S. Grant's capture of Fort Donelson. Two months later, he suffered severe head, thigh and shoulder wounds while leading his regiment in the Hornet's Nest at Shiloh. While recovering, Cruft was promoted to brigadier general of volunteers on July 16. Having healed sufficiently, he resumed command and distinguished himself at the disastrous Battle of Richmond, Kentucky, on August 29–30, where he was again wounded. Cruft again commanded a brigade at Corinth, Mississippi, in early October and was present but not engaged at Perryville, Kentucky, a few days later.

Cruft was in the thick of action during the winter of 1862–63, commanding a brigade of John M. Palmer's division at Stones River and Murfreesboro and then at Chickamauga in September 18–20, 1863. He subsequently was appointed to command a division in General Gordon Granger's IV Corps, which he led at Chattanooga, taking part in the Battle of Lookout Mountain. In 1864, he commanded his division during the Atlanta campaign. At the Battle of Nashville, he led a "provisional division" composed mainly of African American detachments from four separate corps of the Army of the Cumberland who had been unable to rejoin their units in Georgia. On March 7, 1865, President Abraham Lincoln nominated Cruft for promotion to brevet major general of volunteers to rank from March 5; the Senate approved the nomination on March 10. He was mustered out on August 24, 1865.

Cruft returned to Terre Haute and resumed law practice with his prewar partner, Colonel John Baird, who had led the 85th Indiana Infantry. An active Freemason, Cruft was grand commander of the Grand Commandery of Indiana, Knights Templar, in 1873. He died in Terre Haute on March 23, 1883, and was buried at Woodlawn Cemetery.

JEFFERSON COLUMBUS DAVIS

March 2, 1828–November 30, 1879

Jefferson Columbus Davis.
Courtesy Library of Congress.

No relation to the Confederate president, Indiana's Jefferson Columbus Davis was born on March 2, 1828, near Memphis in Clark County. After education at the Charlestown Seminary and harboring dreams of a military career, he received his parents' permission to join the 3rd Indiana Infantry Regiment for the Mexican-American War in 1846. Despite his youth, he distinguished himself in combat at Buena Vista. Two years later, on June 17, 1848, he was commissioned into the Regular Army as a second lieutenant and posted to the 1st Artillery. He was promoted to first lieutenant in 1852. He served in several posts during the 1850s before arriving at Fort Moultrie in Charleston Harbor, South Carolina, in 1858.

Davis was still at Fort Moultrie when Major Robert Anderson arrived and consolidated harbor defenses at Fort Sumter. Confederate batteries opened fire on Sumter on April 12. After a thirty-four-hour bombardment, the garrison surrendered, evacuated the fort and boarded a steamer for New York City. Davis proceeded almost immediately from New York City to Indianapolis, where he offered his services to Governor Oliver

P. Morton, who enlisted his aid in recruiting volunteers. Meanwhile, he was promoted to captain in the Regular Army. After Davis recruited and organized several regiments, Morton appointed him colonel of the 22nd Indiana Infantry in August 1861.

In the fall of 1861, Davis's regiment joined General John C. Frémont's command at Jefferson Barracks near St. Louis, where he organized a brigade. His first combat occurred in October at Lexington, where the brigade was criticized for poor preparation by General John Pope. Davis took the criticism to heart and vowed to never again be caught short for lack of preparation. Promoted to brigadier general of volunteers in December, he commanded a division in General Samuel Curtis's Army of the Southwest at the victorious Battle of Pea Ridge in Arkansas in March 1862 and the Siege of Corinth, Mississippi, in May. His performance in those engagements established his reputation as an aggressive field officer.

Davis's career nearly ended abruptly in late September 1862, during the Confederate invasion of Kentucky, when he murdered General William "Bull" Nelson, his commanding officer, during a feud at the Galt House Hotel in Louisville, just before the Battle of Perryville. Only the intervention of Governor Morton and Louisville attorney James Speed, President Abraham Lincoln's future attorney general, prevented him from going to trial for murder.

Soon restored to command, Davis went on to lead a division at Murfreesboro, Chickamauga and Atlanta and a corps during Sherman's March to the Sea and the Carolinas campaign. His performance normally would have earned promotion to major general. But because of the Nelson murder, he never won further promotion, despite recommendations on his behalf by Generals George H. Thomas and William T. Sherman.

Mustered out of volunteer service in 1866 and appointed colonel of the 23rd Infantry in the Regular Army, Davis served in Alaska and then completed the chastisement of the Modocs in California after the murder of General Edward R.S. Canby in 1873. He died in Chicago on November 30, 1879, and was buried at Crown Hill Cemetery in Indianapolis.

EBENEZER DUMONT

November 23, 1814–April 16, 1871

A Hoosier example of a political general, Ebenezer Dumont was born on November 23, 1814, in the Ohio River village of Vevay, Switzerland County, Indiana. He attended Hanover College and then graduated from Indiana University in Bloomington. After studying law, he was admitted to the bar about 1835 and opened practice in Vevay. At some point, he relocated to Lawrenceburg in neighboring Dearborn County. In 1838, he was elected to a two-year term in the Indiana House of Representatives, following in the footsteps of his father, who had served in both houses of the assembly. He also served for several years as treasurer of both Lawrenceburg

Ebenezer Dumont. *Courtesy Wikimedia Commons.*

and Dearborn County. When the Mexican-American War began, he enlisted in the army, serving as captain and then lieutenant colonel of the 4th Indiana Infantry Regiment.

Dumont returned to Lawrenceburg after the war and resumed his legal and political career. In 1850, he was reelected to the state House of Representatives and served as Speaker. A Democrat at the time, he was an elector for Franklin Pierce in 1852 and president of both the State Bank of Indiana and the State Sinking Fund Commission during much of the 1850s. As sectional tensions increased, he gradually transitioned from Democrat to Whig to Republican and changed his residence to Indianapolis.

With the outbreak of the Civil War, he volunteered his services to Governor Oliver P. Morton, who appointed him colonel of the 7th Indiana Infantry Regiment, a ninety-day unit. In July, Dumont led the regiment well at Laurel Hill, Rich Mountain and Corrick's Ford during George B. McClellan's western Virginia campaign. In September, the regiment reenlisted for three years, and Dumont was made brigadier general of volunteers. In the fall, Dumont led the regiment at Cheat Mountain and on the Greenbrier River against Robert E. Lee. In January 1862, he commanded the 17th Brigade of the Army of the Ohio, and in May, he repulsed John Hunt Morgan's cavalry at Lebanon, Kentucky. Dumont commanded the 12th Division of General Don Carlos Buell's army during the Confederate invasion of Kentucky in the fall of 1862. But the division did not engage at Perryville, remaining instead at Frankfort while part of his division was captured at Hartsville, Tennessee, by troops under Nathan B. Forrest. Dumont took sick leave in December 1862 and resigned his commission on February 28, 1862, having been elected to the U.S. House of Representatives.

Dumont served two terms in Congress, during which he chaired the Committee on the District of Columbia and the Committee on Expenditures in the Department of the Interior. He accepted an appointment by President Ulysses S. Grant as governor of Idaho Territory in 1871, but he died in Indianapolis on April 16 before taking the oath of office. He was buried at Crown Hill Cemetery.

JOHN EDWARDS

October 24, 1815–April 8, 1894

Few Hoosier generals more clearly exemplified the mobility of Civil War–era society than John Edwards. He was born on October 24, 1815, in Louisville, Kentucky. After an education in the local schools, he studied law and was admitted to the Kentucky bar. Although his father was a Kentucky slave owner, Edwards detested slavery. In 1833, after his father died, he moved to Lawrence County, Indiana, where he established a legal practice, freed the slaves and gave them property on which to begin new lives. In 1844, Edwards was elected to the Indiana House of Representatives and served one term. He moved to California in 1849 and was immediately elected an *alcalde*, or local magistrate. But he remained there only three years before returning to Indiana in 1852. He was promptly elected to the state Senate as a Whig, but he served only briefly, moving in 1853 to Charlton, Iowa, where he established a law practice.

Edwards quickly became embroiled in Iowa politics. In 1856, he was elected to the Constitutional Convention that framed a document that was adopted in 1857. That same year, he founded the *Patriot*, a Republican Party newspaper, and in 1858, he was elected to the Iowa House of Representatives. He was reelected in 1860 and chosen as Speaker of the House.

A few weeks after the Civil War began, Edwards was appointed lieutenant colonel and aide on the staff of Governor Samuel J. Kirkwood to protect Iowa's Missouri border from invasion. In August 1862, he was promoted to colonel and given command of the 18th Iowa Infantry, which was assigned to the Army of the Southwest under General John Schofield. The regiment was garrisoned at Springfield, Missouri, during most of 1863, until it was moved to Fort Smith, Arkansas, with Edwards as post commander. In the spring of 1864, the regiment participated in General Frederick Steele's disastrous Camden campaign. On September 24, 1864, Edwards was promoted to brigadier general of volunteers. He subsequently was given command of a brigade and then a division in the District of the Frontier, headquartered at Fort Smith. He remained there until the war ended.

Edwards never received brevet promotion to major general of volunteers, but President Andrew Johnson appointed him assessor of U.S. Internal Revenue Service at Fort Smith, where he had made his home. In 1870, he ran for Congress as a Liberal Republican against the incumbent, Thomas Boles, a former Confederate who ran as a moderate. He received the victor's credentials and served from March 4, 1871, to February 9, 1872, when he was replaced by Boles, who successfully contested the outcome. Edwards remained in Washington, however, where his military and legal experience provided a lucrative income. He died in Washington on April 8, 1894, and was buried at Arlington National Cemetery.

ROBERT SANFORD FOSTER

January 27, 1834–March 3, 1903

Robert Sanford Foster was born on January 27, 1834, in Vernon, Jennings County, Indiana. After receiving his education in the local schools, Foster moved to Indianapolis, where he worked in an uncle's grocery and learned the tinner's trade. When the Civil War erupted, he enlisted as a private in the 11th Indiana Infantry, a ninety-day regiment commanded by Colonel Lewis Wallace, and was quickly promoted to captain. In July, the regiment fought at Rich Mountain during George McClellan's western Virginia campaign. After the battle, Foster was promoted to major and transferred to the 13th Indiana, commanded by Colonel Jeremiah C. Sullivan.

Foster was subsequently promoted to lieutenant colonel and then to colonel in April 1862. He led the regiment in General James Shields's division during General Stonewall Jackson's Shenandoah Valley campaign of 1862. He was then transferred to Suffolk, Virginia, where he commanded a brigade in the Union force defending the town. Foster was advanced to brigadier general of volunteers on June 12, 1863, and participated in General Quincy Gillmore's siege of Charleston, South Carolina, during the fall and winter of 1863–64. In that action, he commanded a brigade that protected the harbor at Folly Island.

Upon completing that duty, Foster served briefly in Florida and then returned to southeastern Virginia, where he rejoined Gillmore, now commander of X Corps in the Army of the James, as his chief of staff. From then until the end of the war, Foster served in the Petersburg campaign, commanding a brigade and then a division in X Corps, which was merged into XXIV Corps in December 1864. On April 2, 1865, his division and that of General John W. Turner made successive assaults on Fort Gregg, the central hinge of the collapsing Confederate lines. Brevetted major general of volunteers, Foster served after the war on the military commission that tried the conspirators in the assassination of President Abraham Lincoln.

Foster resigned his commission on September 25, 1865, and returned to Indianapolis. During the following years, he was elected a city alderman, served for five years as city treasurer and was U.S. marshal for Indiana from 1881 to 1885 under appointments by Presidents James A. Garfield and Chester A. Arthur. He also was elected president of the Indianapolis Board of Trade and served in state positions as a director of the Northern Prison and quartermaster general of the Indiana National Guard. He died in Indianapolis on March 3, 1903.

WILLIS ARNOLD GORMAN

January 12, 1816–May 20, 1876

Willis Arnold Gorman, another example of the mobility of Hoosier generals, was born near Flemingsburg, Kentucky, on January 12, 1816. His family moved to Bloomington, Indiana, when he was nineteen. He studied law and was admitted to the bar, after which he pursued further study at Indiana University, graduating in 1845. Meanwhile, he entered politics, serving as clerk of the Indiana Senate from 1836 to 1837 and Senate enrolling secretary in 1839–40. He was elected to the state House of Representatives from Brown and Monroe Counties in 1840 and served three terms. Upon leaving his seat, he served as Senate secretary during 1845–46.

When the Mexican-American War started, Gorman enlisted in the 3rd Indiana Infantry Regiment and served as a major. He subsequently became colonel of the 4th Indiana Infantry Regiment and saw action at Buena Vista and Puebla. He returned to Indiana after the war, resumed his legal practice and was elected to the U.S. House of Representatives as a Democrat, serving from 1849 to 1853, when President Franklin Pierce appointed him territorial governor of Minnesota. Gorman remained in Minnesota when his term ended, in 1853, and opened a law practice in St. Paul. During the next few years, he served in the state constitutional convention of 1857, was elected to the Minnesota House of Representatives in 1858 and served into 1859 and was an elector for Stephen A. Douglass in the election of 1860.

Willis Arnold Gorman.
Courtesy Library of Congress.

With secession and the Civil War, Gorman offered his services to the State of Minnesota and was appointed colonel of the 1st Minnesota Infantry. He served at First Bull Run on July 21, 1861, where his regiment performed well as part of General William B. Franklin's brigade of General Samuel P. Heintzelman's division. As a result, Gorman was promoted to brigadier general of volunteers on September 7, 1861, and given command of the 1st Brigade of General John Sedgwick's division of Edwin V. Sumner's II Corps in the Army of the Potomac. During George B. McClellan's Peninsula campaign in the summer of 1862, Gorman commanded the brigade effectively at Seven Pines and again at Antietam on September 17. After Antietam, Gorman briefly took command of the division while Sedgwick recovered from battle wounds.

In November 1862, Gorman was assigned to command the District of Eastern Arkansas, headquartered in Helena. Later replaced as district commander by General Benjamin M. Prentice, Gorman remained in the district and participated in minor operations during the Vicksburg campaign. He was mustered out of service on May 4, 1864, and returned to St. Paul, where he resumed his law practice. He was elected city attorney in 1869 and held the position until his death on May 20, 1876. He was buried at Oakland Cemetery in St. Paul.

WALTER QUINTIN GRESHAM

March 17, 1832–May 28, 1895

A distinguished lawyer, soldier, politician and diplomat, Walter Quintin Gresham was born on March 17, 1832, in the Harrison County village of Lanesville. After an early education in a log schoolhouse and May's Seminary in Corydon, he taught school, clerked in various county offices and attended Indiana University. Meanwhile, he read law, and after being admitted to the bar in 1854, he commenced a successful practice in Corydon. He also made a foray into politics, making unsuccessful bids as a Whig for Harrison County prosecuting attorney in 1854 and as a Republican for county clerk in 1858 before winning a seat in the state House of Representatives in 1860.

Walter Quintin Gresham.
Courtesy Library of Congress.

Gresham quickly became a leader in the House, but he disliked and refused to curry favor with Governor Oliver P. Morton, his fellow Republican—the feeling was mutual. Thus, when the Civil War erupted and Gresham sought a military commission, Morton refused him. Gresham responded by enlisting as a private and was soon elected captain by his company. He finally achieved a colonel's commission with the 53rd Indiana Infantry in October 1861.

Gresham's regiment was present but not engaged at Shiloh, but it performed well at Vicksburg as part of General Jacob G. Lauman's 4th Division in XVI Corps. On August 11, 1863, Gresham was promoted to brigadier general and appointed to command a brigade of XVII Corps at Natchez. During the Atlanta campaign, he led the 4th Division until July 20, when a sharpshooter's bullet shattered his knee and terminated his military service. He resigned from the army but departed with a brevet commission as major general of volunteers.

Once able to walk with crutches, Gresham opened a law office in New Albany, Indiana. He also reentered politics, but despite his military service, he was unsuccessful in campaigns for the U.S. House of Representatives in 1866 and 1868 and for the U.S. Senate in 1880. The House losses no doubt stemmed from the fact that he was a Republican running in a strongly Democratic district. Gresham's political fortunes were better on the national level. In 1869, President U.S. Grant appointed him U.S. district judge for

Indiana, a position he held until 1883, when President Chester A. Arthur appointed him postmaster general. He served until September 1884, when Arthur made him secretary of the U.S. Treasury. Less than two months later, Arthur appointed him to the U.S. 7th Circuit Court of Appeals. He served until 1893, when President Grover Cleveland appointed him U.S. secretary of state, a position he held until his death on May 28, 1895. He was buried at Arlington National Cemetery.

WILLIAM GROSE

December 16, 1812–July 30, 1900

Born on December 16, 1812, in Dayton, Ohio, William Grose had a strong family military heritage. His father served in the U.S. Army under William Henry Harrison during the War of 1812; both of his grandfathers fought in the American Revolution; and his paternal grandfather, Jacob Grose, died in the conflict. William's family moved to Fayette County, Indiana, a few months after his birth and relocated to Henry County in 1829. As a youth, he worked as a farm laborer and in a local brickyard. As a young adult, Grose studied law, and upon admission to the bar in 1832, he established a practice in New Castle, which remained home for the rest of his life. Like many attorneys, he became involved in politics, running unsuccessfully for Congress as a Democrat in 1852. As the sectional conflict over the expansion of slavery heated up, he changed parties and served as a delegate to the first Republican National Convention in 1856. In 1860, he was elected judge of the Henry County Court of Common Pleas.

Grose's service on the bench ended abruptly with the outbreak of the Civil War. In October 1861, he was appointed colonel of the 36th Indiana Infantry Regiment, which he recruited and trained. The 36th Indiana was soon assigned to General Don Carlos Buell's Army of the Cumberland, and it was Buell's only unit engaged on the first day at Shiloh, where Grose's horse was shot from under him and he sustained a slight shoulder wound. Shortly thereafter, Grose succeeded the wounded Brigadier General Jacob Ammen in command of an infantry brigade. He fought in every operation of the Army of the Cumberland during the next year, including the Confederate invasion of Kentucky, Vicksburg, Stones River, Chickamauga, Chattanooga, Tullahoma and Lookout Mountain. During 1864, he led his brigade in a continuing series of smaller engagements that formed General William T. Sherman's Atlanta campaign.

In July 1864, Grose was commissioned a brigadier general of volunteers and given command of a brigade in the division of his fellow Hoosier, Major General Nathan Kimball, in Major General Thomas J. Woods's IV Corps. He then joined the Army of the Tennessee's northward pursuit of John Bell Hood, which culminated in that Confederate army's virtual destruction at Franklin and Nashville. Grose was brevetted major general in August 1865 while serving courts-martial duty for the trial of a fellow officer.

Grose remained in the Regular Army for almost a year after the war ended, resigning his commission on January 31, 1866. President Andrew Johnson subsequently appointed him collector of the internal revenue for his part of Indiana, and he served until 1874. Soon after, he accepted a gubernatorial appointment on the commission that administered construction of mental hospitals in Indiana. In 1878, he barely lost a bid for a congressional seat, but he was elected to the Indiana Senate in 1887 and served until 1891, representing Fayette and Henry Counties. He also wrote a history of the 36th Infantry Regiment and participated in its reunions. Grose died at his home in New Castle on July 30, 1900, and was buried at South Mound Cemetery.

PLEASANT ADAMS HACKLEMAN

November 15, 1814–October 3, 1862

The only Indiana general killed in the Civil War, Pleasant Adams Hackleman was born on November 15, 1814, in Franklin County, Indiana. He started adult life as a farmer but also studied law and was admitted to the bar, practicing in Rush County. He was elected Rush County probate judge in 1837 and served until 1841, when he took a seat in the state House of Representatives. He subsequently served as Rush County clerk and ran unsuccessfully for U.S. House of Representatives in 1858. Meanwhile, in 1840, he took up journalism as editor of the *Rushville Republican*. He was a delegate to the 1860 Republican National Convention, which nominated Abraham Lincoln for president, and attended the Washington Peace Conference, which attempted unsuccessfully to negotiate a compromise that might prevent civil war.

When military hostilities commenced, Hackleman offered his services, and Governor Oliver P. Morton appointed him colonel of the 16th Indiana

Infantry Regiment. He and his unit were deployed to the Eastern Theater as part of a brigade assigned to General Nathaniel P. Banks's division, where they participated in the Union disaster at Ball's Bluff. On April 28, 1862, he was elevated to brigadier general of volunteers and dispatched to General Ulysses S. Grant in the Western Theater. Hackleman was given command of the 1st Brigade in General Thomas A. Davies's 2nd Division of the Army of the Tennessee. The division was temporarily assigned to General William S. Rosecrans's Army of the Mississippi near Corinth, Mississippi. The Confederates attacked Rosecrans's army on October 3, creating a gap in the Union line and causing it to fall back. Hackleman tried gallantly to rally his brigade, but he received a mortal wound to the neck. He was taken to the Tishomingo Hotel in Corinth, where he died that evening. His final words reportedly were, "I am dying, but I die for my country." His body was returned to Rushville, where he was buried. The Rush County village of Hackleman is named in his honor.

WILLIAM HARROW

November 14, 1822–September 27, 1872

A relative latecomer to Hoosier identity, William Harrow was born on November 14, 1822, in Winchester, Kentucky. During his childhood, his family moved to Lawrenceville, Illinois, where he was educated in the common schools and studied law. After being admitted to the bar, he struck up a friendship with Abraham Lincoln and traveled the 8th Judicial Circuit with the future president. Harrow's Indiana connection began about 1859 when he moved to Vincennes, in Knox County, and then relocated to Mount Vernon, his wife's home, in Posey County.

When the Civil War erupted, Governor Oliver P. Morton appointed Harrow a captain in the Knox County Invincibles, one of many militia companies that sprang up as war neared. The Invincibles were soon mustered into the 14th Indiana Infantry, organized at Terre Haute, and Harrow rose successively to major, lieutenant colonel and colonel. The regiment's initial service occurred at Cheat Mountain and Greenbrier in western Virginia, but its real baptism of fire came at Antietam, where it fought in Nathan A. Kimball's 1st Brigade of William H. French's 3rd Division of the II Corps. For four bloody hours, the regiment fought within sixty yards of the Rebel line along the Sunken Road and sustained 181 casualties, about half its strength. As the brigade's senior colonel, Harrow led it at Fredericksburg in December. Based on his performance, Kimball sent a letter to President Lincoln asking that Harrow be promoted to brigadier general. Lincoln approved and forwarded the letter to the War Department. But it took no action, and Harrow remained a colonel through the winter.

Harrow received the promotion in April 1863 and took command of the 1st Brigade, 2nd Division of II Corps. He led the brigade at Gettysburg, where on July 2 it opposed Confederate general Richard H. Anderson's attack on the Union lines. Division commander General John Gibbon was wounded during that action, and Harrow became acting commander. The following day, Harrow's force helped repel Pickett's Charge, at a cost of more than 1,600 casualties out of 3,773 in the division.

Gettysburg was the acme of Harrow's military service. Unfortunately, after-battle reports criticized his ill-temper and questioned his ability to inspire soldiers and cooperate with superiors. As a result, he was relieved of command. Through his friendship with Lincoln, Harrow was reinstated to field command in the Western Theater, where he commanded the 4th Division of the XV Corps in the Atlanta campaign. But Harrow's reputation preceded him. In September 1864, after his men expressed resentment of his harsh discipline, his division was disbanded and its regiments were assigned to other brigades and divisions. When prospective superiors—including Oliver O. Howard, William T. Sherman and Winfield S. Hancock—rejected him, he resigned in April 1865 and resumed his law practice in Mount Vernon. He also engaged in politics, first as a Radical Republican and then as a Liberal Republican. On September 27, 1872, he was killed in a train derailment at New Albany while traveling to Jeffersonville to deliver a speech on behalf of presidential candidate Horace Greeley. His body was returned to Mount Vernon for burial at Bellefontaine Cemetery.

MILO SMITH HASCALL

August 5, 1829–August 30, 1904

Born on August 5, 1829, in LeRoy, Genesee County, New York, Milo Smith Hascall moved to Goshen, Indiana, as a teenager and joined three older brothers. He clerked in a store and served as a schoolteacher until receiving an appointment to West Point in 1848. He finished fourteenth among the forty-three graduates of the class of 1852; notable classmates included Major Generals George Crook, Alexander McDowell McCook, Henry W. Slocum and David S. Stanley. Upon graduation, Hascall was posted to artillery service at Fort Adams, which guarded Newport Harbor, Rhode Island. After a year, he became dissatisfied with garrison duty, resigned his commission and returned to Goshen, where he studied law and opened a legal practice. During the rest of the decade, in addition to his legal work, he became a contractor for the Michigan Southern & Northern Indiana Railroad and served as Elkhart County district attorney and county court clerk.

At the outbreak of the Civil War, Hascall offered to serve and was appointed aide-de-camp to Brigadier General Thomas A. Morris, who headed Indiana volunteers. Two months later, he was appointed colonel of the 17th Indiana Infantry and led it at the Battle of Philippi in western Virginia. In December 1861, he was assigned to Louisville, Kentucky, as a brigade commander in General Thomas J. Wood's division in the Army of the Cumberland. His brigade arrived at Shiloh the day after the battle and was sent on to Corinth, Mississippi, which was under siege by General Henry W. Halleck. He was promoted to brigadier general of volunteers on April 26, 1862.

During mid-July, Hascall led his brigade at Murfreesboro, Tennessee. Later in 1862, he was given command of the 1st Brigade in the 1st Division of General Thomas L. Crittenden's corps, which he led at Stones River from December 31, 1862, to January 2, 1863. Wood was wounded during the fight, and Hascall took temporary command of the division. Soon thereafter, Hascall was transferred to Ambrose E. Burnside's Army of the Ohio. For a time, he commanded the Division of Indiana, where he devoted considerable effort to rounding up deserters and crossing swords with Governor Oliver P. Morton over enforcement of measures to curb antiwar activities of so-called Copperheads and Democratic newspapers. In the fall, Hascall participated in the defense of Knoxville, and in the spring of 1864, he commanded the 2nd Division of XXIII Corps in the Atlanta campaign. His performance won praise from Major General John M. Schofield, commander of the Army of the Ohio, who recommended him for promotion to major general. But the recommendation was not acted on, leading Hascall to resign his commission in October. He returned to Goshen, where he resumed his legal practice and entered banking. He subsequently moved to Galena, Illinois, and then to Chicago in 1890, where he entered the real estate business. He died at his home in Oak Park on August 30, 1904, and was buried at Forest Home Cemetery, Forest Park, Illinois.

JOHN PARKER HAWKINS

September 29, 1830–February 7, 1914

A lifelong Hoosier, John Parker Hawkins was born on September 29, 1830, in Indianapolis. He graduated fortieth in the forty-three-member West Point class of 1852, which included his fellow Hoosier and future Union general Milo Smith Hascall. After graduation, he was brevetted a second lieutenant and appointed to the 6th Infantry Regiment. Promotion was so slow at the time that two years passed before he advanced to full-rank second lieutenant and was assigned to the 2nd Infantry. During the balance of the antebellum period, he served mainly on the northwestern frontier, acting as regimental quartermaster from 1858 to 1861.

When the Civil War erupted, Hawkins moved to the Commissary Department. He was stationed briefly in St. Louis as assistant commissary before being elevated to chief commissary of the District of Southwest Missouri and then functioning successively as inspecting commissary of the Department of Missouri, chief commissary of the XIII Corps and eventually chief commissary of the Army of the Tennessee in early 1863. Soon thereafter, Hawkins took ill and spent three months on sick leave. Upon returning to duty, he was assigned to the District of Northeastern Louisiana and given command of a brigade of United States Colored Troops (USCT). Meanwhile, in April 1863, President Abraham Lincoln nominated Hawkins for promotion to brigadier general of volunteers. The Senate returned the nomination a year later; Lincoln resubmitted it on April 2, 1864, and the Senate confirmed Hawkins on April 18. The same month, he was assigned to command the 1st Division of the USCT, based near Vicksburg. Hawkins and his division performed gallantly in the siege and capture of Mobile in March 1865, resulting in his promotion to brevet major in the Regular Army and subsequently to both brevet brigadier and major general in the Regular Army and major general of volunteers.

Mustered out of volunteer service in February 1866, Hawkins remained in the Regular Army after the war and reverted to his regular rank of captain in the Subsistence Department. He finally advanced to major in 1874. He served at various posts, gradually rising to lieutenant colonel in 1889, colonel in March 1892 and brigadier general in December 1892. The latter promotion accompanied his new position as head of the Subsistence Department with the title of commissary general of subsistence. He headed the department until retiring in September 1894. Hawkins returned to Indianapolis and devoted considerable time studying his family genealogy. He died on February 7, 1914, and was buried at Crown Hill Cemetery.

ALVIN PETERSON HOVEY

September 26, 1821–November 23, 1891

Alvin Peterson Hovey.
Courtesy Wikimedia Commons.

As an Indiana Supreme Court justice, congressman, governor, soldier and diplomat, Alvin Peterson Hovey was a truly distinguished nineteenth-century Hoosier. Hovey was born on September 26, 1821, in Mount Vernon, Indiana. He was orphaned by his father's death when he was fifteen. After an education in local common schools, he pursued a dream of becoming a lawyer. For several years, he worked days as a bricklayer and schoolteacher while studying with attorney John Pitcher. He passed the bar in 1843 and entered practice in Mount Vernon. When the Mexican-American War began, he volunteered and was commissioned a lieutenant in a local company, but it saw no service and he soon resumed practice in Mount Vernon.

Hovey's practice flourished during the late 1840s after he successfully settled the estate of the late William Maclure, the distinguished scientist and educational reformer who had helped make New Harmony, the utopian community, a renowned intellectual center during the 1820s. In 1850, he served in the convention that drafted the Indiana Constitution of 1851. After the convention, he was elected Posey County circuit judge, and in 1854, Governor Joseph A. Wright appointed him to the Indiana Supreme Court at age thirty-two. His service lasted less than a year, as he was defeated for election to a full term. After Hovey left the court, President Franklin Pierce appointed him U.S. attorney for Indiana, a post he held until being removed by President James Buchanan in 1858. He changed his political affiliation from Democrat to Republican and ran for the U.S. House of Representatives that fall but was defeated.

When the Civil War started, Hovey organized the 1st Regiment, 1st Brigade of the Indiana Legion, and was appointed its colonel. Three months later, he resigned and was commissioned colonel in the 24th Indiana Infantry. After a brief stint in Missouri, his regiment was attached to a brigade in Lew Wallace's division. At Shiloh, Hovey's gallantry earned him promotion to brigadier general. In the fall, he commanded a brigade in the Department of Eastern Arkansas under General Samuel Curtis, and in February 1863, he was given command of the 12th Division of XIII Corps in General U.S. Grant's Army of the Tennessee. His division performed conspicuously during the Vicksburg campaign, especially at Champion's Hill.

In December 1863, Hovey was reassigned to Indiana to recruit troops. In May 1864, he resumed combat command with a division of the XXIII Corps for William T. Sherman's Atlanta campaign. But he was there barely a month before taking leave to command the Division of Indiana. In that capacity, with a brevet promotion to major general of volunteers, he handled administrative chores, organized new regiments and forwarded them to service and pursued and arrested members of the Sons of Liberty and Knights of the Golden Circle, both secret organizations sympathetic with the Confederacy.

At the war's end, Hovey resigned his commission and accepted an appointment from President Andrew Johnson as U.S. minister to Peru, serving until 1870, when he resumed law practice in Mount Vernon. In 1886, he won a term in the U.S. House of Representatives and was elected governor of Indiana in 1888. He died in office on November 23, 1891, and was buried at Bellefontaine Cemetery in Mount Vernon.

NATHAN KIMBALL

November 22, 1822–January 21, 1898

Nathan Kimball was born on November 22, 1822, in the small town of Fredericksburg in Washington County, Indiana. He obtained his early education at the Washington County Seminary and then moved on to Asbury College (now DePauw University) in Greencastle, Indiana. After graduating, he moved to Independence, Missouri, where he farmed and taught school while studying medicine with his brother-in-law, a local physician.

Kimball practiced medicine in Independence until the Mexican-American War, when he returned home and was appointed captain of the 2nd Indiana Volunteers. The regiment performed poorly at Buena Vista, but Kimball won praise for successfully rallying his company. After being mustered out, he settled in Loogootee, Indiana, and practiced medicine until the Civil War erupted. He again volunteered, raised a company and was appointed captain. In June, Governor Oliver P. Morton appointed Kimball colonel of the 14th Indiana Infantry. The next month, the 14th joined other Indiana

Nathan Kimball. *Courtesy Library of Congress.*

regiments engaged in the western Virginia campaign, seeing action at Cheat Mountain and Greenbrier River. In March 1862, Kimball moved to the Shenandoah Valley, where he distinguished himself at the Battle of Kernstown as commander of the division of Brigadier General James Shields, who had been wounded. Kimball dealt Confederate general Thomas J. "Stonewall" Jackson one of his few defeats in that encounter and won promotion to brigadier general of volunteers the next month.

When Robert E. Lee invaded Maryland later in September, Kimball led the 1st Brigade of General William French's division of II Corps at Antietam. Kimball's brigade, which included the 14th Indiana, lost more than six hundred men, but its performance won it the name "Gibraltar Brigade." Three months later, Kimball and his brigade showed similar energy in a futile attack on Marye's Heights at Fredericksburg, where he was severely wounded. The next summer, after recovering, Kimball was sent west to command a division of XVI Corps at Vicksburg. After the city fell, Kimball served for a time in Arkansas, defending against General Sterling Price's Confederate army and helping to establish a Unionist government. In April 1864, Kimball was relieved of his duties in Arkansas and reassigned to General William T. Sherman's army, where in May he took command of a brigade in IV Corps. After a strong performance at Peachtree Creek, he again received command of a division.

Later that summer, Governor Morton requested Kimball's services back home, where he played a key role in Morton's efforts to suppress the Knights of the Golden Circle in southern Indiana. After a short tour in Indiana, Kimball returned to the field, commanding a division of General George H. Thomas's Army of the Cumberland at Franklin in November and Nashville in December 1864. He was brevetted major general on February 1, 1865.

Kimball joined the Grand Army of the Republic after the war. He also entered politics, serving as state treasurer from 1867 to 1871. He was elected to the state House of Representatives in 1872 and served a year before becoming U.S. surveyor general for Utah Territory, serving from

1874 to 1878. He stayed in the West for the rest of his life, practicing medicine for the U.S. Indian Agency at Fort Hall, Idaho, in 1879 and working as postmaster for Ogden City, Utah, from 1879 to 1883. He died on January 21, 1898, and was buried there.

THOMAS JOHN LUCAS

September 9, 1826–November 16, 1908

Thomas John Lucas. *Courtesy Library of Congress.*

Thomas John Lucas was born on September 9, 1826, in Lawrenceburg, Dearborn County, Indiana. His father, a watchmaker, was a veteran of the Napoleonic wars who had immigrated to the United States after the Battle of Waterloo. Thomas followed his father's trade until 1847, when he volunteered for the Mexican-American War. He was appointed a second lieutenant in the 4th Indiana Infantry Regiment and served for fourteen months. Mustered out in 1848, he returned to watchmaking and pursued the trade until the Civil War. On May 20, 1861, he became a lieutenant colonel in the 16th Indiana Infantry, a one-year regiment commanded by Colonel Pleasant A. Hackleman. His first combat occurred in October 1861 when his regiment covered the retreat of Federal forces during the debacle at Ball's Bluff.

In May 1862, the 16th reenlisted for three years. Hackleman was promoted to brigadier general at the same time, and Lucas was given command of the regiment and advanced to colonel. Lucas and the 16th participated in another Union defeat at Richmond, Kentucky, in August 29–30, 1862, when some two hundred members of the regiment were killed or wounded and six hundred were captured during a confrontation with Confederate troops commanded by General Braxton Bragg. After a subsequent parole and exchange of prisoners, Lucas's command was reorganized, and he was sent west to participate in U.S. Grant's Vicksburg campaign, during which he was wounded three times. While recovering, he returned to Indiana for duty on a military commission that tried several members of the pro-Confederate Sons of Liberty for treason. After that, he was assigned to head a cavalry brigade during General Nathaniel P. Banks's unsuccessful Red River expedition. On November 10, 1864, Lucas was promoted to brigadier general of volunteers and given successive command of a brigade and then a division during the campaign to take Mobile, Alabama. During that duty, he led raids into west Florida, southern Georgia and Alabama. His performance won a brevet promotion to major general of volunteers, effective March 26, 1865. He commanded a cavalry brigade at Vicksburg when the war ended.

Mustered out in 1866, he returned to Lawrenceburg and served in several political posts. He worked for the U.S. Revenue Service from 1875 until 1881 and from 1881 to 1885 as postmaster in Lawrenceburg. He ran unsuccessfully for U.S. House of Representatives as a Republican in 1886. Lucas died on November 16, 1908, and was buried at Greendale Cemetery in Lawrenceburg Township.

MAHLON DICKERSON MANSON

February 20, 1820–February 4, 1895

Born on February 20, 1820, in Piqua, Ohio, Mahlon Dickerson Manson received his early education in local schools and then clerked in a drugstore. In 1842, he moved to Montgomery County, Indiana, where he taught school for a year and took classes at the Ohio Medical School in Cincinnati. But he ultimately abandoned his medical aspirations and instead became a druggist in Crawfordsville. When the Mexican-American War began, Manson volunteered and served as company captain in the 5th Indiana Infantry during 1847–48, seeing action in General Winfield Scott's campaign from Vera Cruz to Mexico City. After the war, Manson returned to Crawfordsville, resumed his career as a druggist and became involved in Democratic politics. He was elected to the state House of Representatives in 1851 and was a delegate to the 1856 Democratic National Convention, which nominated James Buchanan for president.

After the Civil War broke out at Fort Sumter, Manson volunteered for service. Although Manson was a Democrat, Governor Oliver P. Morton personally signed his enrollment and appointed him captain of the Crawfordsville Guards, a company raised by Manson and Colonel Lew Wallace. It was mustered into Wallace's 10th Indiana Infantry as Company G.

Manson rose quickly to major and then to colonel in late May when Wallace advanced to brigadier general. Manson experienced his first combat in July at Rich Mountain in western Virginia. In January 1862, he led a brigade during General George H. Thomas's Union victory over Confederate forces headed by Felix Zollicoffer at Mill Spring in Kentucky. Manson's force was deployed to the Louisville area after the battle and remained there during the spring and summer. Meanwhile, his leadership at Mill Spring earned him a promotion to brigadier general of volunteers on March 24.

Manson did not fare so well the following October, when his green Indiana troops were defeated at Richmond, Kentucky, by Braxton Bragg's invading Confederate army. Manson was wounded, his company suffered heavy casualties and he was captured along with more than four thousand of his men. He was exchanged two months later, and in July 1863, he helped to repel John Hunt Morgan's raid into Indiana and Ohio. For a brief time after the Battle of Chickamauga, Manson commanded the XXIII Corps, but during the Atlanta campaign, he was reduced to command of a brigade in the Army of the Ohio. At Resaca, Georgia, on May 14, 1864, he received a disabling wound from an exploding shell that injured his right shoulder. Realizing that he could no longer exercise field command, he resigned on December 21, 1864, and returned home.

Manson's postwar life involved an array of business, civic and political activity. He served as a director of Citizens National Bank in Crawfordsville, held an interest in the Indiana Wire Fence Company and was on the Purdue University Board of Trustees from 1875 to 1879. He ran for U.S. House of Representatives in 1870, defeating his friend Lew Wallace. He joined the Indiana Democratic Committee in 1873 and was elected chairman in 1875. Manson was elected state auditor in 1876 and lieutenant governor in 1884, but he resigned the latter post in 1886 to become U.S. Internal Revenue collector for the Seventh District. He died on February 4, 1895, at Crawfordsville and was buried at Oak Hill Cemetery.

George Francis McGinnis

March 19, 1826–May 29, 1910

George Francis McGinnis was born on March 19, 1826, in Boston, Massachusetts. His mother died when he was an infant, and he lived with an aunt in Hampden, Maine, until he was eleven. Then his father took him to Chillicothe, Ohio, where the elder McGinnis practiced his trade as a hatter. When the Mexican-American War began, George enlisted and became a lieutenant in the 2nd Ohio Infantry. He served throughout the war and was mustered out as a captain on July 25, 1848.

After the war, McGinnis moved to Indianapolis, where he followed his father's trade and began manufacturing hats. When news of the Confederate attack on Fort Sumter broke, he enlisted as a private in Colonel Lewis Wallace's 11th Indiana Infantry, a three-month regiment. He advanced to lieutenant colonel a few days later and was promoted to colonel when the 11th reenlisted for three years in August. Meanwhile, the regiment saw

George Francis McGinnis.
Courtesy Wikimedia Commons.

limited action in the western Virginia campaign. It was a different story in early 1862, when the regiment saw heavy action at Fort Donelson and Wallace praised McGinnis for the effective leadership of his troops. Two months later, McGinnis temporarily commanded the 1st Brigade of Wallace's division at Shiloh.

On November 29, 1862, McGinnis was promoted to brigadier general of volunteers and given command of the 2nd Brigade of the 2nd Division of the Department of East Arkansas, which he headed during the early winter of 1862–63. In February 1863, he took command of the 1st Brigade, 12th Division of General John McClernand's XIII Corps for the Yazoo Pass expedition against Vicksburg. The attack was a fiasco, mainly because of McClernand's ineptness, and McGinnis's reputation among Regular Army officers was tarnished. After Vicksburg, he held a series of minor commands, mainly in Nathaniel P. Banks's Department of the Gulf. He was mustered out on August 24, 1865, and returned to Indianapolis, where from 1867 to 1871 he was Marion County auditor. He served several other local and state offices until 1900, when President William McKinley appointed him postmaster for Indianapolis. He died on May 29, 1910, and his ashes were interred at Crown Hill Cemetery.

JAMES WINNING MCMILLAN

April 28, 1825–March 9, 1903

James Winning McMillan was born on April 28, 1825, in Clark County, Kentucky. Something of a rolling stone, McMillan served first as a sergeant of the 4th Illinois Infantry and then as a private in a Louisiana volunteer battalion during the Mexican-American War. After his discharge in 1848, he moved to Indiana and engaged in several different enterprises at various locations during the next dozen years.

When the Civil War erupted, McMillan helped organize the 21st Indiana Infantry and was appointed its colonel. In the spring of 1862, McMillan's regiment was assigned to General Benjamin F. Butler's army of occupation in New Orleans, and on August 5, his unit suffered 126 casualties in defending

James Winning McMillan.
Courtesy Library of Congress.

Baton Rouge against attack by Confederates commanded by former vice president John C. Breckinridge. McMillan also engaged in the disreputable cotton trade in the La Fourche District. A month after the Baton Rouge battle, elements of McMillan's regiment were ambushed by Confederates near Boutte Station and Bayou des Allemands.

On April 4, 1863, McMillan was promoted to brigadier general of volunteers, to rank from November 29, 1862. He subsequently joined General Nathaniel P. Banks's Army of the Gulf, commanding a brigade in the 1st Division of General William Emory's XIX Corps. From March through May 1864, McMillan participated in the disastrous Red River campaign, during which he performed well at Mansfield, Pleasant Hill and Monett's Ferry. Meanwhile, McMillan advanced to divisional command, and in July 1864, he moved with the XIX Corps to General Philip Sheridan's army in the Shenandoah Valley in Virginia. McMillan fought well at Winchester and at Cedar Creek, where he helped repulse an attack by Confederate general Jubal Early that threatened to rout Sheridan's entire army. After the Valley campaign, McMillan commanded the 1st Division in the Department of West Virginia until the end of the war. He was brevetted major general in March 1865 and resigned his commission in May. True to his wandering nature, McMillan moved to Kansas after the war. In 1875, he was appointed to the Pension Office Board of Review in Washington, D.C., and held the position until his death on March 9, 1903. He was buried at Arlington National Cemetery.

SOLOMON MEREDITH

May 29, 1810–October 2, 1875

Solomon Meredith was born on May 29, 1810, in Guilford County, North Carolina, the youngest of ten children of David and Mary Meredith. His grandfather James Meredith fought at the Revolutionary War battle of Guilford Courthouse. His Quaker parents, who educated their children at home, opposed slavery and were conductors on the Underground Railroad. When he was nineteen, Solomon moved to Wayne County, Indiana, where he worked as a laborer to further his education. A born leader, he entered politics and was elected county sheriff at age twenty-four. After two terms, he won four terms in the Indiana House of Representatives, serving until 1849, when he was appointed U.S. marshal for the District of Indiana. He served until 1853. Originally a Whig, he transitioned to the Republican Party in the 1850s. Along with his political

Solomon Meredith. *Courtesy Wikimedia Commons.*

activities, he was a farmer and transportation promotor, serving as financial agent for the Indiana Central Railroad and director of the Cincinnati & Chicago Railroad and the Whitewater Canal.

At the outbreak of the Civil War, Meredith sought a commission from Governor Oliver P. Morton. When Morton moved slowly, Meredith raised a regiment on his own and asked President Lincoln to intervene on his behalf. While Meredith's initiative irritated him, Morton ultimately appointed Meredith colonel of the 19th Indiana Infantry. Meredith reciprocated by supporting Morton in his rivalry with Republican congressman George W. Julian. The 19th Indiana was incorporated with three Wisconsin regiments to create the so-called Black Hat Brigade, commanded by General John Gibbon. It distinguished itself at Second Bull Run in August 1862, where Meredith was severely wounded and his regiment took heavy casualties. While Meredith recovered in Washington, D.C., Gibbon again led the brigade at Antietam, where the 19th Indiana again suffered heavy losses. Gibbon resented Meredith's absence and asserted that he should be stripped of his command. But politics prevailed. Meredith's performance at Second Bull Run won him promotion to brigadier general on October 6. One month later, Gibbon was promoted to divisional command, and Meredith took leadership of the brigade, now called the "Iron Brigade of the West."

Meredith first led the Iron Brigade at Fredericksburg, where he crossed swords with division commander General Abner Doubleday, who temporarily relieved him of command. But Meredith returned in time to lead the brigade at Chancellorsville and then at Gettysburg, where on the first day of combat he received a wound that incapacitated him until November. In early 1864, he was assigned to a garrison post at Cairo, Illinois, followed in September by a similar position at Paducah, Kentucky, where he remained until the end of the war. He was brevetted a major general on August 14, 1865, and mustered out on August 24.

After the war, he was appointed surveyor general of the Montana Territory and served for two years. He retired to his farm near Cambridge City in Wayne County in 1867 and devoted himself to breeding and raising prize livestock. He died at his home on October 2, 1875, and was buried at Riverside Cemetery.

John Franklin Miller

November 21, 1831–March 8, 1886

John Franklin Miller was born on November 21, 1831, in South Bend, Indiana. He attended schools in South Bend and Chicago and then studied law at Ballston Spa Law School in Saratoga, New York, receiving his degree at age twenty-one. Miller began practicing in South Bend but moved to Napa, California, in 1853. There he continued in practice and was quickly elected county treasurer. His Golden State sojourn was brief, however, as

John Franklin Miller. *Courtesy Library of Congress.*

he returned to South Bend in 1855 and was elected to the Indiana Senate in 1861.

When the Civil War began, Miller left the Senate and on August 27, 1861, was commissioned colonel of the 29th Indiana Infantry. The regiment saw its first major service at Shiloh as part of General Edward N. Kirk's brigade in General Alexander McD. McCook's division of the Army of the Ohio. From there, the regiment deployed to Mississippi for the Siege of Corinth and then trailed Braxton Bragg's Confederate army through northern Alabama and Tennessee into Kentucky.

In late December 1862, Miller commanded a brigade in General James Negley's division at the Battle of Stones River. On the second day of the battle, Miller was wounded in the neck while spearheading the Union counterattack that drove back a Confederate attack led by General John C. Breckinridge. Miller was wounded again on June 27, 1863, when he lost his left eye in a minor skirmish at Liberty Gap during the Tullahoma campaign. The injury put him out of commission for nearly a year. Finally, he was promoted to brigadier general of volunteers on April 10, 1864, to rank from January 5, and was assigned to administrative duty as garrison commander at Nashville in May 1864. His last command occurred in December when he led a large force of infantry and artillery at the Battle of Nashville. He was brevetted a major general of volunteers on March 13, 1865.

When the war ended, Miller declined a commission as a colonel in the Regular Army and left the army on September 29, 1865. He relocated to California when President Andrew Johnson appointed him collector of customs at the Port of San Francisco, a post he held for four years. Turning his attention to business, he served for twelve years as president of the Alaska Commercial Company, which dominated the fur industry in the recently acquired Pribilof Islands, and pursued development interests in the Napa Valley. He reentered politics in 1878 as a member of the state constitutional convention. Two years later, the legislature elected him to the U.S. Senate, where he staunchly opposed Chinese immigration and supported the Chinese Exclusion Act of 1882. He died in office on March 8, 1886, and was buried at Laurel Hill Cemetery in San Francisco; his remains were reinterred at Arlington National Cemetery in 1913.

ROBERT HUSTON MILROY

June 11, 1816–March 29, 1890

Robert Huston Milroy. *Courtesy Library of Congress.*

Robert Huston Milroy was born on June 11, 1816, on a family farm near Salem in Washington County, Indiana. When he was ten, his family moved to Carroll County, where he lived until about 1840, when he enrolled at Captain Partridge's Academy, a military school in Norwich, Vermont, where in 1843 he earned a Bachelor of Arts degree and a Master of Military Science degree. Three years later, he offered his training to the nation, serving as a captain in the 1st Indiana Volunteers during the Mexican-American War. Mustered out in 1847, without ever seeing action, he studied law at Indiana University in Bloomington and graduated in 1850. Upon admission to the bar, he entered practice in Rensselaer, Indiana. He soon entered politics and served briefly as a judge before resuming private practice in 1854.

As the Civil War neared, Milroy recruited a company from among men in the Rensselaer vicinity, and just two weeks after the attack on Fort Sumter, he was mustered into the Union army as colonel of the 9th Indiana Infantry, a three-month unit. When its initial tenure expired, the regiment reenlisted for three years in July and participated in Federal operations in western Virginia. On September 3, 1861, Milroy was promoted to brigadier general of volunteers and given command of the Cheat Mountain district in western Virginia. On March 10, 1863, he advanced to major general, retroactive to November 29, 1862. Meanwhile, Milroy fought in the Shenandoah Valley campaign and commanded a brigade of the I Corps in General John Pope's Army of Virginia at Second Bull Run. In June 1863, as Milroy commanded a division that guarded the north end of the Shenandoah near Winchester, he was overwhelmed by Confederate general Richard Ewell's corps of the Army of Northern Virginia, which was heading to Pennsylvania. A court of inquiry exonerated Milroy of responsibility for the disaster, but he never again held field command. During the last year of the war, he served under General George H. Thomas at Nashville, where he organized and assigned militia regiments.

Milroy resigned on July 26, 1865, and returned home to Indiana, where he served as a trustee of the Wabash and Erie Canal Company. In 1872, he was appointed superintendent of Indian Affairs for the Washington Territory. After three years in that post, he served for a decade as Indian agent in Olympia, Washington. Meanwhile, Milroy suffered increasingly intense pain from the hip wound he received at Winchester. He died in Olympia on March 29, 1890, and was buried at Masonic Memorial Park at Tumwater, Washington. Citizens of Rensselaer later erected a bronze statue in his honor at Milroy Park near downtown.

WILLIAM ANDERSON PILE

February 11, 1829–July 7, 1889

One of a handful of generals whose primary connection to Indiana was their birthplace, William Anderson Pile was born on February 11, 1829, near Indianapolis. His parents moved to Missouri while he was a small child and settled in St. Louis. After receiving his secondary education, he studied for

William Anderson Pile. *Courtesy Wikimedia Commons.*

the ministry in the Methodist Episcopal Church and eventually became a pastor in the Missouri Conference. When the Civil War began, he enlisted as a chaplain in the Union army; he was attached to the 1st Missouri Light Artillery and commissioned a lieutenant on June 12, 1861. The next year, he transitioned from chaplain to combat officer, becoming captain of Battery I of the 1st Missouri on July 31, 1862, and posted near Corinth, Mississippi. One month later, he was promoted to lieutenant colonel of the 33rd Missouri Infantry, a command nicknamed the "Merchants' Regiment" because it had been raised by the Merchants Exchange of St. Louis.

On December 23, 1862, Pile was promoted to colonel of the 33rd Missouri and moved it to Arkansas. Most of its work involved garrison duty, but it did take part in the March 1863 expedition assigned to find a back door to Vicksburg by way of the Yazoo River. After that mission, he assumed garrison duty at Helena, Arkansas, on the Mississippi River and held that post until January 1864. Meanwhile, he was promoted to brigadier general of volunteers on December 26, 1863, giving him distinction as the only Union general who also was an ordained minister. In early 1864, he took command of a brigade of African American troops based at Benton Barracks in St. Louis and led them in the campaign against Mobile as part of General John P. Hawkins's African American division. In April 1865, he was brevetted major general of volunteers for gallantry during the capture of Fort Blakely, Alabama.

Mustered out in August, Pile was elected to Congress as a Radical Republican in 1866 and served one term. After Pile was defeated in 1868, President Ulysses S. Grant appointed him territorial governor of New Mexico, a post he held until 1871, when Grant designated him minister to Venezuela. He later moved to Monrovia, California, and began cultivating grapes. He died on July 7, 1889, and was buried at Live Oak Cemetery in Monrovia.

THOMAS GAMBLE PITCHER

October 23, 1824–October 21, 1895

A native Hoosier, Thomas Gamble Pitcher was born on October 23, 1824, in the Ohio River town of Rockport in Spencer County, Indiana. When he was seventeen, he received an appointment to the U.S. Military Academy at West Point. He ranked fortieth in the forty-one-member class of 1845, which included ten future Union generals. Assigned as a brevet second lieutenant to the 5th Infantry, he participated in the occupation of Texas before the Mexican-American War and was brevetted first lieutenant for gallantry in action. He transferred to the 8th Infantry in 1849 and was promoted to captain in 1858.

When the Civil War broke out, Pitcher was stationed as commissary officer at Fort Bliss outside El Paso, Texas. Transferred back east, he was promoted to major and given command of a battalion in General Henry

Prince's brigade, which was part of General Christopher C. Augur's division of General Nathaniel P. Banks's corps. Pitcher experienced his only field command when the brigade skirmished with Confederates at Cedar Mountain in August 1862, just before Second Bull Run. During the battle, he received a severe knee wound that rendered him an invalid for several months and unfit for further field service. Promoted to brigadier general of volunteers, effective November 29, 1862, he returned to duty in June 1863 and was appointed acting assistant provost marshal general in Vermont. In October 1864, he was reassigned to Indiana as provost marshal general and charged to oversee recruitment of new troops. He was so effective that only 2,082 draftees were required to fill a December 1864 call for 22,582 men.

Pitcher remained in Indianapolis when the war ended and was appointed military commander of the District of Indiana on September 25, 1865. He held that post until August 17, 1866, when he returned to the Regular Army as colonel of the 44th Infantry Regiment and superintendent of West Point. The latter appointment made him the lowest-ranking graduate ever to head West Point. Upon completion of that duty in 1871, he became governor of the Soldiers' Home in Washington, D.C., and served until 1877. He retired the next year due to his war wound. He subsequently moved to Fort Bayard, New Mexico, where he died on October 21, 1895. He was interred at Arlington National Cemetery.

Hugh Thompson Reid

October 18, 1811–August 21, 1874

An exemplar of the geographic mobility of the Union army general officer corps, Hugh Thompson Reid was born of South Carolina parents in Union County, Indiana, on October 18, 1811. He received a common school education and then studied law at Indiana University in Bloomington. After passing the bar, he moved to Fort Madison, Iowa, where he served from 1840 to 1842 as prosecutor for a five-county district in the southeast corner of the state. For the rest of the decade, he continued to practice law while acquiring large tracts of land and engaging in railroad development. In 1849, he moved to Keokuk, where he was elected president of the Des Moines Valley Railroad, a post he held through the first year of the Civil War.

In early 1862, Reid raised the 15ᵗʰ Iowa Infantry regiment in Keokuk, and on February 22, he was commissioned its colonel. Once the regiment was mustered in, Reid led it to St. Louis, where it was incorporated into the Army of the Tennessee at Pittsburg Landing, Tennessee, for the Battle of Shiloh. There the regiment was assigned initially by General U.S. Grant to prevent stragglers from leaving the field. But in short order, it was attached to General Benjamin Prentice's division, which was heavily engaged near the Hornet's Nest. Reid was severely wounded in the neck and presumed dead. Remarkably, his body was taken to the rear, where he regained consciousness and briefly rejoined the fighting. But the injury ultimately put him out of action until October, when he took command of a brigade in the Army of Tennessee for the Battle of Corinth. However, he fell ill and was unable to exercise battlefield command.

On January 18, 1863, in preparation for Grant's Vicksburg campaign, Reid was appointed to command a brigade of African American and white troops in the XVII Corps, stationed near Lake Providence, Louisiana. Reid had previously advocated enlisting Black troops, observing with a strong racist overtone that "every colored soldier who stops a rebel bullet saves a white man's life." Meanwhile, General Grant had noticed his gallantry at Shiloh and recommended him for promotion to brigadier general of volunteers, which was awarded on March 13, 1863. In June, Reid's brigade engaged Confederate general Richard Taylor, son of former general and President Zachary Taylor, who was attempting to relieve pressure on Vicksburg. The following October, after Vicksburg fell, Grant dispatched Reid to southern Illinois, where he commanded the District of Cairo. He resigned his commission on April 14, 1864, returned to Keokuk and resumed the presidency of the Des Moines Valley Railroad. Reid died of kidney disease on August 21, 1874, and was buried at Oakland Cemetery.

JOSEPH JONES REYNOLDS

January 4, 1822–February 25, 1899

A native of Flemingsburg, Kentucky, where he was born on January 4, 1822, Joseph Jones Reynolds moved with his family to Lafayette, Indiana, when he was fifteen. In 1838, he entered Wabash College in Crawfordsville. He received an appointment to West Point the next year and ranked tenth among the thirty-nine graduates in the class of 1843. His classmates included thirteen other Union army generals, including his close friend U.S. Grant.

Assigned to the 4th U.S. Artillery, he served garrison duty at various posts in Virginia, Pennsylvania and Texas before the Mexican-American War. In 1846, Reynolds returned to West Point, where he taught for eight years. He so enjoyed his instructional duties that in 1857 he resigned his commission as a first lieutenant and accepted a position

Joseph Jones Reynolds. *Courtesy Library of Congress.*

as professor of mechanics and engineering at Washington University in St. Louis while also engaging in the grocery business in Lafayette. When Civil War hostilities erupted in April 1861, Reynolds was appointed colonel in the 10th Indiana Legion regiment and then promoted to brigadier general of Indiana Volunteers. His state service was brief. On June 14, 1861, he was appointed brigadier general of U.S. Volunteers to rank from May 17. He was quickly assigned to command a brigade in northwestern Virginia, where in September he repulsed a Confederate attack at Cheat Mountain, helping to win that part of Virginia for the Union.

In January 1862, Reynolds again resigned his commission when his brother and partner in the Lafayette grocery business died, making it necessary for him to take over its operations. While conducting the business, however, he used his military skills to recruit and organize state units. In August, he rejoined the service as colonel of the 75th Indiana Infantry, and the next month he was recommissioned brigadier general. On November 29, he was promoted to major general and given command of a division in XIV Corps of the Army of the Cumberland. On June 24, 1863, he led the division at Hoover's Gap, the main battle of the Tullahoma campaign, in which General William S. Rosecrans expelled Braxton Bragg's Confederate army from central Tennessee. On October 10, Reynolds became chief of staff to General George H. Thomas, commander of the Army of the Cumberland. He served in that capacity during the Battle of Chickamauga and the Siege of Chattanooga. In January 1864, he was placed in command of the New Orleans defenses. Six months later, he received command of the XIX Corps in the Army of the Gulf and aided General Edward R.S. Canby in organizing the attack on Mobile. From November 1864 to April 1866, he led the Department of Arkansas.

Reynolds reverted to colonel after the war and took command of the 26th Infantry. He was successively brevetted brigadier general and major general. He moved to the cavalry in 1870 and served until 1872, when he returned to regimental command. Meanwhile, the Texas legislature elected him to the U.S. Senate, but he lost the seat when another candidate contested the outcome. After returning to the infantry, he was given successive assignments in Nebraska and Wyoming. On March 17, 1876, while leading the advance corps of General George Crooks's expedition against the Sioux in the Powder River area of Montana, his troops attacked a village in a battle that resulted in numerous casualties. His premature retreat triggered a court-martial and led to his resignation. He moved to Washington, D.C., where he died on February 25, 1899, and was buried at Arlington National Cemetery.

LOVELL HARRISON ROUSSEAU

August 4, 1818–January 7, 1869

Lovell Harrison Rousseau.
Courtesy Library of Congress.

A Kentucky native who made a mark in Indiana and then became the only general commissioned by a city, Lovell Harrison Rousseau was born on August 4, 1818, in Stanford, Lincoln County, Kentucky. His father died when Lovell was fifteen, so he quit school and went to work as a laborer on a turnpike being built in central Kentucky. After a while, he moved to Lexington and read law. In 1840, he relocated to Bloomfield, Indiana, where he was admitted to the bar in 1841. Just three years later, he was elected to the Indiana House of Representatives, representing Greene County. When the Mexican-American War began, he joined the 2nd Indiana Volunteer Regiment as a captain, serving during 1846–47.

After the war, Rousseau resumed practice in Bloomfield and was elected to the Indiana Senate, beginning in 1847. He moved his practice to Louisville, Kentucky, in 1849 and submitted his resignation from the Senate, but it was rejected, so he served until 1850. In 1860, he was elected to the Kentucky Senate. A staunch Unionist, he resigned when the Civil War began and started recruiting volunteers for the Union. Since Kentucky had declared neutrality, Rousseau and his allies had to proceed gingerly. On May 25, 1861, the city government authorized creation of two regiments of Home Guard, dubbed the Louisville Legion, commanded by Rousseau as brigadier general. Rousseau recruited the troops and stationed them at Camp Joe Holt in Clarksville, Indiana. Once Kentucky declared for the Union, Rousseau resigned his city commission and, in September 1861, was mustered into federal service as colonel of the 3rd Kentucky Infantry. On October 1, he was promoted to brigadier general of volunteers.

Rousseau saw his first combat at Shiloh, where he commanded a brigade in Don Carlos Buell's Army of the Ohio. At Perryville, he led a division and performed brilliantly, earning promotion to major general on October 8, 1862. He subsequently transferred to General George H. Thomas's Army of the Cumberland, where he exercised divisional command at Murfreesboro in the Tullahoma campaign and at the end of the Chickamauga campaign. In July 1864, as commander of the District of Tennessee and under orders from General William T. Sherman, he mounted a highly successful, four-hundred-mile cavalry raid through northern Alabama to destroy Montgomery & West Point Railroad. He later led similar raids across Mississippi and western Tennessee.

Rousseau resigned from the army after the war and was immediately elected to the U.S. House of Representatives as a Radical Republican. But his views soon moderated, and he supported the conservative policies of President Andrew Johnson. During intense debates about the powers of the Freedmen's Bureau, he lost his temper with Iowa representative Josiah B. Grinnell and caned him in a Capitol corridor. Censured and forced to resign, he was resoundingly reelected and served until July 1866. He reentered the Regular Army as a brigadier general and was brevetted major general on March 28, 1867. He was sent to Alaska, where he formally received its transfer from Russia to the United States. In 1868, he succeeded General Philip Sheridan in command of the Department of Louisiana, headquartered at New Orleans. He died there on January 7, 1869, and was buried at Arlington National Cemetery.

James Murrell Shackelford

July 7, 1827–September 7, 1909

A wartime Indiana adoptee, James Murrell Shackelford was born in Lincoln County, Kentucky, on July 7, 1827. He attended schools in Springfield and Stanford. When he was twenty, he enlisted in Company I, 4th Kentucky Volunteers, for service in the Mexican-American War. He was elected first lieutenant and was mustered out in 1848. After the war, he studied law and was admitted to the Kentucky bar in 1853. For several years, he conducted a successful practice in Louisville, which no doubt brought him numerous connections with neighboring southern Indiana.

In the fall of 1861, after the Civil War began, Shackelford began recruiting troops for the 25th Kentucky Infantry Regiment for Union service, and he was commissioned its colonel on January 1, 1862. Integrated into Charles Cruft's brigade of Lew Wallace's division, the regiment fought at Fort Donelson, sustaining eighty-four casualties. In March 1862, shortly before the Battle of Shiloh, Shackelford was forced to resign his commission because of poor health. In August, after months of convalescence, he recruited the new 8th Kentucky Cavalry and was appointed its colonel on September 13, 1862. On March 17, 1863, he was promoted to brigadier general, effective January 2. With the promotion came nominal command of the 1st Brigade, 2nd Division, of the XXIII Corps. But he still headed the 8th Kentucky, and his main service of the year occurred in July, when he and General Edward Hobson pursued Confederate general John Hunt Morgan on his long raid through Kentucky, Indiana and Ohio, where he finally accepted Morgan's surrender near Wellsville, Ohio, on July 26. Later in 1863, under the command of General Ambrose E. Burnside, Shackelford participated in the capture of the Cumberland Gap during the East Tennessee campaign, where he commanded a cavalry division in the XXIII Corps, and at Knoxville, where he led the Cavalry Corps in the Department of the Ohio.

Shackelford resigned from military service in January 1864, after the death of his wife, and resumed law practice, now relocated to Evansville, Indiana. He remained in the Hoosier State until 1889, when he was appointed U.S. judge for the Indian Territory in Muskogee, now Oklahoma, where he subsequently became attorney for the Choctaw nation. He died on September 7, 1909, at his summer home in Port Huron, Michigan. His body was moved to Louisville, Kentucky, where he was buried at Cave Hill Cemetery.

JAMES RICHARD SLACK

September 28, 1818–July 28, 1881

James Richard Slack was born on September 28, 1818, in Bucks County, Pennsylvania. He received his basic education at an academy at Newton, Pennsylvania. In 1837, his family moved to Delaware County, Indiana, where he labored on his father's farm while also teaching school and studying law. He was admitted to the bar on September 28, 1840, his twenty-second birthday, and moved a few weeks later to Huntington, Indiana, where he set up a legal practice. When he arrived, he had only six dollars in cash and the clothes he was wearing. Slack quickly made a name in politics, being elected Huntington County auditor in 1842. He served in that position until 1851, when he took a seat in the Indiana Senate, representing Huntington and Wells Counties. In 1854, he ran unsuccessfully for U.S. House of Representatives and returned to the state Senate, this time representing Huntington and Whitley Counties in the 1859 and 1861 sessions.

Slack was still in the Senate when the Civil War broke out, but he left his seat and began organizing the 47th Indiana Volunteer Infantry, based in Anderson. The regiment was mustered in on December 13, 1861, with Slack as its colonel. The regiment's first action was at New Madrid and Island No. 10, where Slack commanded a brigade in General John Palmer's 3rd Division in General John Pope's Army of the Mississippi. Slack subsequently led his regiment during several expeditions on the Mississippi River, including the White River expedition and the Yazoo Pass engagement. He later fought at Champion's Hill and in the Siege of Vicksburg, where he led a brigade in the division headed by his fellow Hoosier, General Alvin P. Hovey. After Vicksburg, he moved to the Department of the Gulf, where he remained through the end of the war. During this period, he played a minor role in the Red River expedition and commanded the 2nd Brigade in the 2nd Division of XIX Corps. He was promoted to brigadier general of volunteers on November 10, 1864, and brevetted major general by President Andrew Johnson in July 1866 to rank from March 13, 1865. At the end of the war, he commanded the 1st Brigade of the 1st Division in XIII Corps, which he led at the Battle of Fort Blakely.

Slack remained in the army for several months after war and was appointed to command Brazos Santiago, Texas. He stayed until October 1865, when he accompanied the 47th Indiana back home to be mustered out. He himself was mustered out in January 1866. After leaving service, Slack resumed law practice in Huntington. In 1873, Governor Conrad Baker appointed him judge of the new 28th Judicial Circuit, and he won election to the seat in 1878. He was defeated in 1880 in a Congressional bid. On July 28, 1881, while visiting Chicago, he suffered a fatal heart attack and was buried at Mount Hope Cemetery in Huntington.

JEREMIAH CUTLER SULLIVAN

October 1, 1830–October 21,1890

Jeremiah Cutler Sullivan.
Courtesy Indiana Supreme Court.

Jeremiah Cutler Sullivan was born on October 1, 1830, in Madison, Indiana. His father was Jeremiah C. Sullivan, a former Indiana legislator and state Supreme Court judge who also had the distinction of naming the state capital Indianapolis. Appointed to the U.S. Naval Academy, the younger Sullivan graduated in 1848, was commissioned an ensign and served on four different vessels during the next six years. He resigned his commission in 1854 and returned to Indiana to study law. Upon passing the bar, he commenced private practice in Indianapolis.

At the outbreak of the Civil War, Sullivan aided in recruitment and organization of the 6th Indiana Infantry, a three-month unit based in Indianapolis. He was commissioned a captain and fought with the regiment at Philippi in western Virginia on June 3. When the 6th Regiment was mustered out, Sullivan was appointed colonel of the 13th Indiana and led it at Rich Mountain. During the Shenandoah Valley campaign in 1862, he headed a brigade in General James Shields's division at Kernstown and was commissioned brigadier general of volunteers as of April 28. Shortly thereafter, he took command of a brigade of General William S. Rosecrans's Army of the Mississippi and led it at Iuka and Corinth. In the fall of 1862, he was given command of scattered garrison troops in the District of Jackson, Tennessee, and took on the challenge of battling the raiders of Confederate general Nathan B. Forrest.

Sullivan demonstrated his moral fiber in late December 1862 when he received General U.S. Grant's General Order No. 11 demanding the expulsion of Jews from his district. Sullivan refused to execute the command, asserting that he "was an officer of the army and not of a church." He ultimately was forced to carry out the order, but on January 4, President Lincoln revoked Grant's order. Nevertheless, Sullivan subsequently served as Grant's inspector general early in the Vicksburg campaign, and after the fall of the city, he became chief of staff for General James B. McPherson.

Relieved of command in the West in September 1863, Sullivan resumed duty in the Department of West Virginia under General Benjamin F. Kelley, his father-in-law, who was a former Baltimore & Ohio Railroad official now assigned to guard the vital transportation artery. The following summer, General Philip Sheridan took command of the area that included the Department of West Virginia, leaving Sullivan without a command assignment. For reasons that are not clear, Sullivan apparently rubbed superiors the wrong way, and he was denied a brevet promotion to major general after his resignation from service in May 1865.

After the war, Sullivan relocated to General Kelley's home in Oakland, Maryland, but he did not resume legal practice. He moved to Oakland, California, in 1878, but again he did not practice law, accepting an assortment of clerical positions instead. He died in Oakland on October 21, 1890, and was buried at Mountain View Cemetery.

JAMES CLIFFORD VEATCH

December 19, 1819–December 22, 1895

James Clifford Veatch was born on December 19, 1819, in the tiny Harrison County, Indiana town of Elizabeth. His family had a military and political heritage. His grandfather fought at King's Mountain, and a great-grandfather died at Camden during the American Revolution. His father, Isaac Veatch, was an Indiana state legislator. James Veatch received his early education in common schools and from private tutors. He studied law and was admitted to the Indiana Bar in 1840. About the same time, he moved to the Ohio River town of Rockport in Spencer County. In 1841, he was elected county auditor, an office he held until 1855, when he was defeated for reelection. He lost a race for U.S. House of Representatives the following year as a Republican, but he remained in politics, serving as a delegate to the 1860 Republican National Convention, and being elected to the Indiana House of Representatives the same year.

Veatch had just begun his legislative term when the Civil War erupted, and he held on to his seat while joining the Union army as colonel of the 25th Indiana Infantry on August 19, 1861. The regiment's first combat service occurred at General U.S. Grant's capture of Fort Donelson in February 1862. At Shiloh in early April, Veatch commanded a brigade in General Stephen Hurlbut's division, and his four regiments experienced 630 casualties. He was promoted to brigadier general of volunteers later that month and subsequently led the brigade at the Siege of Corinth and during Hurlbut's move on Memphis. In the months that followed, Veatch commanded the District of Memphis and was involved in several minor battles, including Hatchie's Bridge, where he was wounded in an engagement with Confederate troops under Sterling Price and Earl Van Dorn.

After leading the 4th Division of XVI Corps, Army of the Tennessee, during the Meridian expedition, his division joined General William T. Sherman's army for the Atlanta campaign, fighting at Resaca, Dallas and Kennesaw Mountain. Just before the Battle of Atlanta, he went on sick leave. While recuperating, he incurred the ire of General Oliver O. Howard, who had instructed him to remain in Memphis and await orders after returning from leave. As a result, he remained without a command until February 1865, when he was assigned to the Department of the Gulf and given command of a division in General Gordon Granger's XIII Corps for the capture of Mobile. His performance earned a brevet to major general of volunteers. He then commanded a district in West Louisiana until August, when he was mustered out.

Veatch returned to Rockport after the war and was appointed Indiana adjutant general in 1869. The next year, he was appointed collector of internal revenue by President Grant, a post he held until 1883. He was a delegate to the 1884 Republican National Convention, lost a race for presidential elector the same year and served on the Republican State Central Committee. He died on December 22, 1895, and was buried at the Sun Set Hill Cemetery in Rockport.

GEORGE DAY WAGNER

September 22, 1829–February 13, 1889

George Day Wagner. *Courtesy Library of Congress.*

George Day Wagner was born on September 22, 1829, in Ross County, Ohio. In 1833, the family moved to a farm in Warren County, Indiana. George received his basic education at local public schools and worked on the farm while studying law. After admission to the bar, he entered politics as a Republican and was elected to the Indiana House of Representatives in 1856, representing Warren County. In 1858, he was elected to the Senate and served in the 1859 and 1861 sessions. Meanwhile, he stumped vigorously for Abraham Lincoln in 1860 and served as president of the Indiana Agricultural Society.

When the Civil War erupted, he offered his services and was appointed colonel of the 15th Indiana Infantry, organized in Lafayette. After brief service in western Virginia, he led a brigade of Major General Don Carlos Buell's Army of the Ohio at Shiloh, where he won a commendation by General Thomas J. Wood, his division commander. His services warranted promotion to brigadier general of volunteers on April 4, 1863, to rank from the previous October. In the fall of 1863, as commander of the 21st Brigade in Major General William S. Rosecrans's army, he performed gallantly at Murfreesboro and Chickamauga, where he commanded the post at Chattanooga. At Missionary Ridge in November 1863, Wagner's brigade lost more than seven hundred members while driving General Braxton Bragg's Confederate troops from the mountain. Wagner's service continued into 1864, during the Atlanta campaign, when he commanded the 2nd Brigade in IV Corps, sustaining heavy losses at Kennesaw Mountain.

Wagner's active military service ended abruptly after the Battle of Franklin, Tennessee, on November 30, 1864. He commanded a division in IV Corps of Major General George H. Thomas's Army of the Cumberland and was ordered to provide rear guard for General John M. Schofield's retiring forces. Wagner's immediate superior, Brigadier General Jacob D.

Cox, ordered him to withdraw as Confederates under John Bell Hood advanced on his position. Wagner stood his ground instead; as a result, his position was overrun, and two of his brigades were routed. Cox accused Wagner of disobeying orders, prompting his request to be relieved of duty, citing his wife's serious illness. Wagner returned to Indianapolis to await further orders. Except for a brief assignment in St. Louis, those orders never came. Wagner was mustered out in August 1865, and his wife died less than a year later. After her death, he opened a law office in Williamsport, Warren County. He also resumed the Indiana Agricultural Society presidency and vigorously publicized modern agricultural methods. He died suddenly in Indianapolis on February 13, 1889, and was buried at Armstrong Cemetery near Greenhill, Warren County.

LEWIS "LEW" WALLACE

April 10, 1827–February 15, 1905

Author, lawyer, journalist, jurist, politician and diplomat, Lewis "Lew" Wallace was born on April 10, 1827, in Brookville, Indiana. His family moved to Indianapolis in 1837 after his father, David Wallace, was elected governor of Indiana. Young Wallace exhibited early interest in history, politics, law and religion. After graduating from Wabash College in Crawfordsville, he studied law and was admitted to the bar in 1849. Meanwhile, he was a reporter for the *Indianapolis Daily Journal* during 1844–45 and served in the Mexican-American War as a second lieutenant in the 2nd Regiment, Indiana Volunteers, during 1846–47. In 1848, he edited a Free-Soil paper, and from 1851 to 1853, he was prosecuting attorney for the Indiana 8th Circuit. In 1856, he was elected to the Indiana Senate, representing Montgomery County, and served from 1857 to 1859.

Immediately after the attack on Fort Sumter, Governor Oliver P. Morton appointed Wallace to the crucial position of state adjutant general, and he was commissioned colonel of the 11th Indiana, a three-month unit, on April 25, 1861. Four months later, the regiment reenlisted for three years. After service at Romney in western Virginia, Wallace was promoted to brigadier general of volunteers on September 3, 1861. During the winter of 1862, he fought under General U.S. Grant in the capture of Fort Henry and Fort Donelson, where his performance led to promotion to major general, effective March 21, 1862, making him the youngest major general in the Union army. Unfortunately, for reasons not primarily his fault, Wallace's military standing was tarnished a few weeks later when he got lost and arrived late at Shiloh on the first day. His division played a major role in driving back the Confederates on the second day, but heavy Union losses ignited a whispering campaign against Wallace within Grant's staff, even though the latter placed no blame on the Hoosier. In June 1862, Wallace served as military governor of Memphis and then asked for a leave from the army.

Upon returning to service in the fall, General-in-Chief Henry W. Halleck, who looked after Regular Army officers, blocked Wallace from another major command.

Lewis Wallace. *Courtesy Library of Congress.*

Instead, he removed to Cincinnati, where he mobilized the defense of the city against an anticipated attack by the forces of Confederate general Edmund Kirby Smith. Wallace's preparation apparently so impressed Confederate spies that the attack did not occur. Later, President Lincoln appointed Wallace to an administrative post based in Baltimore, and in the summer of 1864, he halted General Jubal Early's advance on Washington at Monocacy River.

In 1865, Wallace served on the military commission that examined the charges against General Don Carlos Buell for dereliction of duty in Kentucky in 1862 and then chaired the military trial of Major Henry Wirz for war crimes as commander of the Andersonville prisoner of war camp. After the war, he resumed law practice in Crawfordsville, ran unsuccessfully for Congress and served successively as territorial governor of New Mexico and U.S. minister to the Ottoman Empire. His greatest claim to fame, however, was as a novelist, most notably his bestseller *Ben-Hur: A Tale of the Christ*, published in 1880. He died in Crawfordsville on February 15, 1905, and was buried at Oak Hill Cemetery.

August von Willich

November 19, 1810–January 22, 1878

August von Willich. *Courtesy Wikimedia Commons.*

Indiana's only foreign-born, full-rank Civil War general, August von Willich was born on November 19, 1810, in Braunsberg, Prussia. His father had fought in the Napoleonic Wars, and young August was educated at military schools in Potsdam and Berlin. He entered the Prussian army as a lieutenant in 1828 and advanced to captain three years later. During the liberal revolutionary movement that swept Europe in 1846–48, Willich adopted the teachings of Karl Marx and submitted his resignation from the army. However, the resignation letter's subversive content triggered his arrest and court-martial. But he was acquitted and allowed to resign. During 1848 and 1849, he took an active part in the revolution as a leader of a Free Corps in the Baden-Palatinate uprising. Among his associates were Franz Sigel and Carl Schurz, who also became leading German American politicians and Union generals. When the continental revolutions failed, Willich immigrated to London, where he learned the carpenter's trade and engaged in an anti-Marxian movement that considered Marx too conservative.

In 1853, Willich moved to the United States, settling initially in Brooklyn, where he found work in the Brooklyn Navy Yard. Still an ardent communist, he moved to Cincinnati in 1858 and edited a German-language newspaper. Upon the outbreak of the Civil War, he recruited some 1,500 German immigrants for service in the 9th Ohio Infantry. He served as its adjutant with the rank of first lieutenant before being promoted to major in June 1861, and in July, he led his troops at Rich Mountain in western Virginia. But his tenure with the 9th Ohio was brief. A short time later, he received an invitation from Indiana governor Oliver P. Morton to command the 32nd Indiana Infantry, a German American regiment being organized in the state capital. Willich was a tough drillmaster, but he cared for his troops, who nicknamed him "Papa."

Willich's regiment won national acclaim when a small detachment held off 1,300 of Terry's Texas Rangers and infantry at Rowlett's Station,

Kentucky, in November 1861. At Shiloh the next April, he demonstrated strong leadership on the second day, when he stabilized his unsteady regiment after it came under heavy fire and then led it in a successful bayonet charge. On July 17, 1862, he was promoted to brigadier general of volunteers and given command of the 6th Brigade, 2nd Division, in the Army of the Ohio. He distinguished himself at Perryville and again at Murfreesboro, where he was captured after his horse was shot from under him. He was paroled and exchanged in time to command a brigade in Alexander McCook's XX Corps at Chickamauga. He then participated in General William T. Sherman's Atlanta campaign and was wounded in the shoulder at Resaca. Upon recovery, he took command of a combined post at Cincinnati, Ohio, and Covington and Newport Barracks, Kentucky. He served until the end of the war, when he was mustered out and brevetted major general in October 1865.

Willich returned to Ohio after the war and was elected Hamilton County auditor. But he served only three years before the Franco-Prussian War lured him back to Germany, where he offered his services to Kaiser Wilhelm I. The king politely declined because of Willich's age. He stayed in Berlin for a time, attending lectures by Karl Marx and earning a degree in philosophy at the University of Berlin. He later returned to Ohio and established residence in St. Mary's, Auglaize County. He died in Cincinnati on January 22, 1878, and was buried at Elmwood Cemetery.

Francis Asbury Shoup, CSA

March 22, 1834–September 4, 1896

Francis Asbury Shoup, the only Confederate general born in Indiana and one of a handful of northern nativity, was born into a wealthy merchant family in Laurel, Franklin County, on March 22, 1834. He studied briefly at Asbury College (now DePauw University) in Greencastle and then moved on to West Point. He graduated fifteenth among the thirty-four members of the class of 1855, which boasted two Confederate and seven Union generals. Upon graduation, Shoup was assigned as a second lieutenant to the 1st U.S. Artillery Regiment and stationed in Florida during the Third Seminole War. After five years of service, Shoup resigned his commission, studied law and was admitted to the bar in Indianapolis in 1860. He also joined a militia unit that became a Union army company. But in 1861, he moved back to Florida and was admitted to the bar in St. Augustine.

Apparently because of his admiration for the South's aristocratic traditions and manners, he adhered to the Confederacy and offered his services to Florida governor Madison S. Perry. He was commissioned a lieutenant in the state artillery and given command of a battery at Fernandina. In October 1861, he joined the Confederate army, was promoted to major and was sent to the Trans-Mississippi Department. After a brief stint in that post, he was assigned to Kentucky, where he led a twelve-gun battalion of Arkansas artillery. By the spring of 1862, he was artillery chief for Major General William J. Hardee. He performed brilliantly in that capacity at Shiloh, massing cannon fire on the Union salient called the "Hornet's Nest." After promotion to brigadier general on September 12, 1862, he joined the staff of General Thomas C. Hindman as assistant adjutant general and saw action at Prairie Grove, Arkansas, in December.

In early 1863, Shoup served as artillery chief for General Simon B. Buckner in the defense of Mobile, after which he took command of a Louisiana infantry brigade that served with Major General John C. Pemberton during the Siege of Vicksburg. Captured when the city fell in July 1863, he spent several months in prison. But he was paroled in time to become artillery chief for Lieutenant General Joseph E. Johnston during the Georgia campaign of 1864. His skillful preservation of the artillery during successive retreats and the strength of the defensive works along the Chattahoochee River drew praise from his superiors. When General John Bell Hood replaced Johnston, Shoup became his chief-of-staff.

After the war, Shoup pursued a career in education and religion. In 1865, he was elected chair of the Mathematics Department at the University of Mississippi, and in 1868, he entered the Episcopal ministry, serving initially as rector of St. Peter's Parish in Oxford. In 1869, he moved to Sewanee: The University of the South, in Tennessee, as mathematics professor and chaplain. He remained until 1875 and served parishes in both the South and North during the next eight years. He returned to Sewanee in 1883 as professor of mathematics and engineering and served until his death on September 4, 1896, at Columbia, Tennessee. He was interred at Sewanee.

BREVET GENERALS

WILLIAM A. ADAMS

September 23, 1839–April 4, 1874

William A. Adams was born on September 23, 1839, in the small town of Greeneville, Davidson County, Tennessee. At some point, he moved to Indiana, where he was living when the Civil War erupted. He was twenty-one when he was commissioned a second lieutenant in Company C of the 22nd Indiana Infantry, which was being organized in Madison and commanded by Colonel William G. Wharton. He was promoted to first lieutenant the following December. During 1862, Adams fought with his regiment at the Battles of Pea Ridge, Perryville and Stones River and was commissioned regimental adjutant on November 30. The regiment remained in the Western Theater during 1863, fighting at Chickamauga and Chattanooga. Adams was promoted to major on August 5, 1864, during the Atlanta campaign, and served with the 22nd until January 1, 1865, when he was mustered out. The next month, he was commissioned a colonel and given command of the new 145th Indiana Infantry, a one-year regiment organized at Indianapolis. The regiment served the balance of the war and postwar occupation duty in Georgia until it was mustered out at Cuthbert, Georgia, on January 21, 1866. He was brevetted brigadier general of volunteers by President Andrew Johnson, to date from March 13,

1865, for gallantry. After the war, he made his residence at Morgantown, Morgan County, Indiana, where he died on April 4, 1874. He was buried at East Hill Cemetery.

DeWitt Clinton Anthony

May 25, 1828–March 15, 1891

DeWitt Clinton Anthony was born on May 25, 1828, in New Albany, Indiana. He attended Anderson Seminary in New Albany and then studied law at the University of Louisville. He graduated in 1851 and lost a race for state representative the same year. He became city attorney the following year and served until 1856. After the Civil War broke out, he joined the Union army in August 1861 and was commissioned a lieutenant colonel in the 23rd Indiana Infantry Regiment, which was organized in New Albany and commanded by Colonel William Sanderson. Attached to the Army of the Tennessee, the regiment fought at Shiloh in April 1862. Because of his legal skills, Anthony subsequently was appointed the regiment's provost marshal general. After Union forces captured Memphis, Tennessee, Anthony was appointed to the same position for the city. He moved to field command in September 1862, when he was promoted to colonel and given charge of the 66th Illinois Volunteer Infantry. He led the regiment until March 1864, when he resigned his commission and was mustered out of service. He was brevetted brigadier general of volunteers in March 1865. After leaving the service, he resumed legal practice in New Albany, where he died on March 15, 1891. He was interred at Fairview Cemetery.

Orion Alexander Bartholomew

September 4, 1837–September 17, 1919

Orion Alexander Bartholomew was born on September 4, 1837, in the small town of Belleville, located on the National Road near Danville, Hendricks County, Indiana. After his early education, he attended Indiana Asbury University (now DePauw University) in Greencastle, Indiana. He was there when the Civil War erupted, and he immediately enlisted as a sergeant in Company A, 7th Indiana Infantry, a three-month regiment commanded by Colonel Ebenezer Dumont. After fighting at Philippi, Virginia, he was discharged in August and immediately joined the 70th Indiana Infantry, commanded by Colonel Benjamin Harrison, a future president of the United States. He was successively promoted to second lieutenant and first lieutenant and served with the regiment until October 1863. When the Lincoln administration authorized the recruitment of African American troops, Bartholomew offered to serve in that branch and was appointed lieutenant colonel in the 15th U.S. Colored Regiment. For the next several months, the regiment served guard duty in Nashville, Columbia and Shelbyville, Tennessee. In 1864, he went to Nashville to organize the 101st U.S. Colored Troops. In June 1864, he was commissioned colonel of the 109th Colored Infantry and ordered to Louisville, Kentucky, from which the unit marched to Virginia and engaged in siege duty at Petersburg and Richmond through the end of the war. Bartholomew was brevetted brigadier general of volunteers on March 13, 1865, for meritorious service during the conflict.

After the war, Bartholomew became a successful attorney in Charlton, Iowa, where he practiced until moving to Minneapolis, Minnesota. He died there on September 17, 1919, and was buried at Lakewood Cemetery.

WILLIAM HENRY HARRISON BEADLE

January 1, 1838–November 13, 1915

William Henry Harrison Beadle was born on January 1, 1838, in Parke County, Indiana. He studied engineering at the University of Michigan, graduating in 1861. When the Civil War erupted, he enlisted in the Union army and was appointed a captain in the 31st Indiana Volunteer Infantry Regiment, which was organized at Terre Haute and commanded by Colonel Charles Cruft. He soon transferred to the 1st Michigan Volunteer Regiment and was promoted to lieutenant colonel. A subsequent wound necessitated his resignation, but in May 1864, he resumed service as a major in the Veterans Reserve Corps, created by the War Department in April 1863 to make suitable military use of disabled soldiers unfit for field duty but capable of garrison or other light duties. He was brevetted brigadier general of volunteers in March 1865.

Beadle studied law at the University of Michigan after the war, but instead of entering law practice, he devoted his career to education and government service. In 1869, President U.S. Grant appointed him surveyor-general of the Dakota Territory, a position that taught him a great deal about land law and the efficacy of land value in financing services such as education. Upon leaving that post in 1879, he was elected territorial superintendent of public instruction and served until 1886. Principles he had learned as surveyor-general shaped the long-term development of educational policy in the Dakotas and other northern plains states. In 1889, he was appointed president and professor of history at South Dakota State Normal School at Madison. He served as president until 1905 but continued as a professor until retiring in 1912. He died on November 13, 1915, while visiting his daughter in San Francisco. His remains were returned to his adopted home in Albion, Michigan, and buried at Riverside Cemetery.

Thomas Warren Bennett

February 16, 1831–February 2, 1893

Thomas Warren Bennett was born on February 16, 1831, in Union County, Indiana. He was educated in the county common schools and then studied law at Indiana Asbury University (now DePauw University) in Greencastle. After graduating in 1855 and upon admission to the bar, he joined the practice of Judge John Yaryan in Liberty, Indiana. Like many other lawyers of his time, he entered politics and was elected to the Indiana Senate in 1859 to complete the term of his mentor, Judge Yaryan. He resigned when the Civil War began, enlisted in the Union army and raised a company for the 15th Indiana Infantry. He was immediately commissioned a captain and was promoted to major in the 69th Indiana Infantry in October. In 1862, he was advanced to regimental command with the rank of colonel. The regiment was assigned to General U.S. Grant's command and fought at Memphis and the Siege of Vicksburg. After its surrender, Bennett led the 69th in the Red River campaign, and he was brevetted brigadier general of volunteers on March 5, 1865.

Bennett returned to Indiana after the war and was again elected to the Indiana Senate and served during two sessions. He moved to Richmond, Wayne County, in 1868 and was elected mayor of Richmond the following year. In 1871, President Grant appointed him governor of the Idaho Territory, and he served until December 5, 1875. He was elected territorial delegate to the U.S. House of Representatives in 1874 and served from 1875 until June 23, 1876. He returned to Indiana after leaving Congress and was again elected mayor of Richmond, serving from 1877 to 1883 and from 1885 until 1887. He died in Richmond on February 2, 1893, and was buried at Earlham Cemetery.

LEWIS JACKSON BLAIR

December 29, 1829–June 10, 1913

Lewis Jackson Blair was born on December 29, 1829, in Ohio. At some point, he moved to DeKalb County, Indiana, where he was living when the Civil War began. In August 1862, he joined the 88th Indiana Infantry Regiment, which was being organized at Fort Wayne under the command of Colonel George Humphrey. The regiment was mustered in on August 29 and immediately dispatched to Louisville to defend the city against an anticipated attack by General Edmund Kirby Smith. On October 1, the regiment joined the pursuit of General Braxton Bragg, during which it experienced its first action at Perryville.

The following year, attached to Major General William S. Rosecrans's Army of the Cumberland, the 88th was heavily engaged at Stones River and Chickamauga, during which Blair's performance won a brevet promotion to major. In 1864, Blair and the 88th Indiana joined Major General William T. Sherman's army for the Atlanta campaign, fighting at Resaca, Dallas and Kennesaw Mountain, as well as in numerous other skirmishes. Later that year, the regiment helped pursue General John Bell Hood into Tennessee and then participated in Sherman's March to the Sea and the Carolina campaign, during which it engaged Joseph E. Johnston's army at Bentonville, North Carolina. The regiment proceeded from there through Goldsboro and Richmond to Washington, D.C., where it mustered out on June 7.

Meanwhile, Blair's leadership merited a brevet promotion to colonel and then to brevet brigadier general of volunteers on March 13, 1865. He returned to Waterloo in DeKalb County after the war. He resided there until his death on June 10, 1913, and was buried at Waterloo Cemetery.

Thomas Jefferson Brady

February 12, 1839–April 22, 1904

Thomas Jefferson Brady was born on February 12, 1839, in Muncie, Indiana, where his father, John Brady, was the first mayor. He graduated from Indiana Asbury University in Greencastle and taught school for several years while studying law. He was admitted to the bar in 1860. When the Civil War began, Brady entered the Union army as a captain in the 8th Indiana Infantry, commanded by Colonel William P. Benton. Promoted to major in May 1862, he served with the regiment until September 28, 1863, when he transferred to the newly organized 117th Indiana Infantry as its commander with the rank of colonel. He served with the 117th in East Tennessee until October 1863, when it was mustered out. In mid-1864, he took command of a new, one-year regiment, the 140th Indiana, with which he saw combat in Tennessee and North Carolina until the end of the war. He was brevetted brigadier general of volunteers in March 1865 for his meritorious service.

Brady returned to Muncie after the war, resumed law practice and became involved in Republican politics. In 1870, President Grant made him consul to St. Thomas in the Virgin Islands. He served until 1875, when Grant appointed him collector of internal revenue for Ohio and Indiana. In 1876, the president named him second assistant postmaster-general. In that post, he was implicated in a scheme in which postal officials received bribes in exchange for awarding delivery contracts in several areas. President Rutherford B. Hayes kept Brady in office, but he resigned in 1881 and was indicted and found guilty of fraud in 1882. However, the judge set aside the verdict, and the defendants were found not guilty on retrial. After his exoneration, Brady moved to Jersey City, New Jersey, where his son was in business. He died there on April 22, 1904, and was buried at Arlington National Cemetery.

Thomas McClelland Browne

April 19, 1829–July 17, 1891

Thomas McClelland Browne was born on April 19, 1829, in New Paris, Ohio, where he was educated in the common schools. His family moved to

Winchester, Randolph County, Indiana, in 1844. For the next four years, he served as a merchant's apprentice and attended a semester at the Randolph County seminary. Meanwhile, he read law and was admitted to the bar in 1849. He immediately plunged into politics and was elected Randolph County prosecuting attorney in 1852. He was elected prosecutor for the 13th Judicial Circuit in 1855 and reelected in 1857 and 1859. He was appointed secretary of the Indiana Senate in 1861 and elected in 1863 to fill a vacant seat in that body.

When his Senate term ended, Browne helped organize the 7th Indiana Volunteer Cavalry, commanded by Colonel John P.C. Shanks. Browne took the field as a captain in August 1863 and was promoted to lieutenant colonel in October. After a brief attachment to the 106th Indiana Infantry, the 7th Cavalry joined with the 119th Indiana Infantry and served the remainder of the war with General Benjamin Grierson's cavalry corps, conducting raids in Tennessee and Mississippi. Browne was promoted to colonel on October 10, 1865, and then brevetted brigadier general of volunteers, retroactive to March 13, 1865.

Browne resumed his legal and political life after the war. He was appointed U.S. attorney for Indiana in 1869 and served until 1872. He defeated Benjamin Harrison for the Republican gubernatorial nomination the same year but lost in the general election to Thomas A. Hendricks. He was elected to the U.S. House of Representatives in 1877 and served until 1891. He died in Winchester on July 17, 1891, and was buried at Fountain Park Cemetery.

GEORGE PEARSON BUELL

October 4, 1833–May 31, 1883

A cousin of Major General Don Carlos Buell, George Pearson Buell was born on October 4, 1833, in the Ohio River town of Lawrenceburg, Indiana. Educated in engineering and military science at Norwich University in Vermont, where he graduated in 1856, he accepted the post of city engineer in Leavenworth, Kansas. He later engaged in gold mining and civil engineering in Colorado. When the Civil War began, Buell returned to Indiana, and in December 1861, he was commissioned a lieutenant colonel in the 58th Indiana Infantry. Buell took command in June 1862 and was promoted to colonel. He led the regiment at Perryville and at Stones River in late December 1862 and early January 1863. During the battle, he took command of the brigade of Brigadier General Milo S. Hascall, who was appointed to lead a division whose commander had been wounded. After the battle, Buell received formal brigade command, and during 1863 and 1864, he commanded several brigades in the Army of the Cumberland. In early 1865, he was brevetted brigadier general of volunteers in honor of his effective management of disassembled pontoon trains used to build bridges to span waterways. He subsequently led brigades in the Army of Georgia through the end of the war.

Buell remained in the military after the war, joining the Regular Army as a lieutenant colonel in the 29th Infantry. On March 2, 1867, he was brevetted colonel as a reward for his leadership at Missionary Ridge during the war. On December 3, 1867, President Andrew Johnson nominated him as brevet brigadier general in the Regular Army, and the Senate ratified the nomination on February 14, 1868. Buell moved to the 11th U.S. Infantry in March 1869. He was promoted to colonel a decade later and given command of the 15th U.S. Infantry. He died on May 31, 1883, while on duty in Nashville, where he was buried at Mount Olivet Cemetery.

Thomas Harvey Butler

November 30, 1833–December 8, 1912

Thomas Harvey Butler was born on November 30, 1833, in Vernon, Jennings County, Indiana. Butler entered wartime service on July 20, 1862, as a captain and company commander in the 76th Illinois Volunteer Infantry. About six weeks later, he transferred to the 5th Indiana Volunteer Cavalry, also as a company commander. He served with the regiment through the rest of the war, fighting in the Knoxville campaign and the Atlanta campaign, including the Battles of Resaca, Dallas, New Hope Church, Allatoona and Kennesaw Mountain. Butler advanced steadily during his service, being promoted to lieutenant colonel in December 1862 and to colonel and regimental commander in December 1863. He was brevetted brigadier general of volunteers on March 13, 1865, for gallantry during the campaigns of 1863 and 1864. He was mustered out on June 27, 1865. He died on December 8, 1912, in Baltimore, Maryland, and was buried at Crown Hill Cemetery in Indianapolis.

JOHN COBURN

October 27, 1825–January 28, 1908

John Coburn was born on October 27, 1825, in Indianapolis, Indiana. He attended Marion County Seminary and then enrolled at Wabash College in Crawfordsville. After graduating in 1846, he studied law, was admitted to the bar in 1849 and opened a practice in Indianapolis. He soon entered politics and was elected to the state House of Representatives in 1850. After one term, he was appointed deputy clerk of the Indiana Supreme Court. He became judge of the 24th District Court of Common Pleas in 1859 and served until 1861, when he resigned and volunteered for military service during the Civil War.

On September 16, 1861, Coburn was commissioned colonel of the 33rd Indiana Infantry, which he had organized. The regiment saw its first combat at Wildcat Mountain in Laurel County, Kentucky, on October 21, 1861, when Union forces turned back a Confederate invasion of southeast Kentucky led by General Felix Zollicoffer. Coburn was captured during a subsequent Kentucky engagement and held at Libby Prison in Virginia before being exchanged. He resumed command of the 33rd Indiana after being exchanged and commanded a brigade during General William T. Sherman's Atlanta campaign. His troops were the first to enter the city and received its surrender. Coburn was mustered out on September 20, 1864, and later brevetted brigadier general of volunteers, effective March 1865.

Coburn resumed his law practice in Indianapolis and served briefly as a circuit judge. He was elected to the U.S. House of Representatives in 1866 and served four terms. After leaving Congress, he was appointed to the Supreme Court of the Montana Territory and served until 1885, when he returned to law practice in Indianapolis. He died there on January 28, 1908, and is buried at Crown Hill Cemetery.

SILAS COLGROVE

May 24, 1816–January 13, 1907

Silas Colgrove was born on May 24, 1816, in Woodhull, New York, where he was educated in the local schools. He arrived in Winchester, Randolph

County, Indiana, in 1837, studied law and was admitted to the bar in 1839. Entering politics as a Whig, he was elected justice of the peace and served until 1844. In 1852, he became prosecuting attorney for the 7th Circuit Court and served until 1856, when he was elected to the Indiana House of Representatives.

Colgrove held the seat until the Civil War erupted in 1861, when he was appointed lieutenant colonel of the 8th Indiana Infantry, a three-month unit that fought at Rich Mountain in western Virginia. He subsequently became colonel and commander of the 27th Indiana Infantry. After wintering in Maryland, the regiment fought in the Shenandoah Valley, seeing action at Front Royal and Winchester. The 27th saw heavy combat at Antietam, where Colgrove had his horse killed from under him, but he escaped injury. He was wounded at Chancellorsville in May 1863 but recovered in time to resume command at Gettysburg. In 1864, he moved to the XX Corps and fought in the Atlanta campaign, sustaining a wound at Peachtree Creek. He was brevetted brigadier general of volunteers on August 7, 1864. In the fall of 1864, he served on the military commission that tried Dr. William Bowles and Lambdin P. Milligan for treason. He resigned his commission in December.

Colgrove returned to Winchester and was elected judge of the 7th Circuit in 1865. He served until 1871, was elected judge of the 25th Circuit two years later and served until 1879. Meanwhile, he became president of the Cincinnati, Fort Wayne & Grand Rapids Railroad. In 1888, he moved to Washington, D.C., for a position in the Pension Office. He resigned for poor health in 1893 and died on January 13, 1907, in Kerr Lake, Florida, where he was buried.

HENRY GREENE DAVIS

June 15, 1819–August 26, 1898

Henry Greene Davis was born on June 15, 1819, in Middlebury, Vermont. His family eventually moved to Kingsville, Ohio, where he attended high school. In 1838, he relocated to Elkhart County, Indiana, where he farmed and operated a sawmill. Active in politics, first as a Whig and then as a Republican, he was elected a justice of the peace in 1859.

When the Civil War started, he joined the 29th Indiana Infantry, organized at LaPorte, and was commissioned a first lieutenant. The regiment was mustered in on August 27, 1861, and joined General Lovell Rousseau's command at Camp Nevin, Kentucky. The regiment fought at Bowling Green in February 1862 and Shiloh in April, with Davis being promoted to captain in March and subsequently to major. For the rest of the year, Davis fought with the 29th Indiana at the Siege of Corinth, Mississippi; moved with General Don Carlos Buell's army in northern Alabama and Tennessee as it repelled Braxton Bragg's forces from Kentucky; and participated in General William S. Rosecrans's campaigns at Murfreesboro and Stones River. During 1863, Davis fought at Tullahoma and later at Chattanooga and Chickamauga. In September 1864, Davis was promoted to lieutenant colonel and transferred to the 101st U.S. Colored Infantry Regiment, then being organized in Tennessee. The unit mustered in on September 16, 1864, and Davis led it until it was mustered out in 1866. He was brevetted brigadier general of volunteers on March 13, 1865.

Davis returned to Elkhart County after the war, and in 1868, he was elected to the Indiana House of Representatives, where he served one term. He later moved to Cheboygan, Michigan. He died on August 26, 1898, in Forest Glen, Montgomery County, Maryland, and was buried at Pine Hill Cemetery in Cheboygan, Michigan.

RICHARD PATTEN DEHART

January 1, 1832–June 12, 1918

Richard Patten DeHart was born on January 1, 1832, in Mason, Warren County, Ohio. In 1855, he relocated to Logansport, Indiana, where he taught school and studied law before his admission to the bar in 1858. He served briefly as prosecuting attorney before being elected in 1860 to the Indiana Senate as a Republican, serving during the 1861 session.

DeHart resigned his seat when the Civil War erupted, enlisted in the 46th Indiana Infantry Regiment as a private and was quickly commissioned first lieutenant and adjutant. In his first year of service, the regiment fought at New Madrid, Island No. 10 and Fort Pillow, Tennessee. In October 1862, DeHart was promoted to lieutenant colonel and transferred to the 99th Indiana Infantry, with which he served during General U.S. Grant's Vicksburg campaign. He returned to Indiana in September 1863 and spent several months on recruiting duty before being commissioned colonel of the new 128th Indiana Infantry in March 1864. In May, the unit joined General William T. Sherman's army for the Atlanta campaign. DeHart was severely wounded on June 6 and sent back home to recover. While there, he served on the commission that tried Lambdin P. Milligan and William Bowles for treason in Indianapolis. DeHart was brevetted brigadier general of volunteers in March 1865 and mustered out the following month.

DeHart returned to Lafayette after the war and established a successful criminal law practice before again serving as prosecuting attorney in 1885–86 and as Tippecanoe County Circuit Court judge from 1901 to 1914. Deeply interested in history, he wrote his monumental *Past and Present of Tippecanoe County, Indiana*, published in 1909. He died in Lafayette on June 12, 1918, and was buried at Spring Vale Cemetery.

GEORGE FREDERICK DICK

February 22, 1829–November 12, 1914

George Frederick Dick was born on February 22, 1829, in Tiffin, Seneca County, Ohio. When he was two, his parents moved to Cincinnati, where he attended a public school. At age sixteen, he joined the Cincinnati Cadets, a youthful military company that taught military organization and discipline. He showed leadership qualities that resulted in his appointment as captain. After finishing his education, he spent twelve years as a tobacconist in the Queen City before opening a similar shop in Attica, Indiana.

When the Civil War began, Dick closed his business, helped organize a three-month company and became its captain. When they offered their services to Governor Oliver P. Morton, he rejected them because the state had oversubscribed its first call for volunteers. The company responded successfully to a second call for troops, and Dick was mustered in on July 22, 1861, as its captain in 20th Indiana Infantry. The 20th performed its first service guarding the Northern Central Railroad in Maryland. During the next year, Dick saw action at the Seven Days Battles and Second Bull Run, leading to promotion to major in August 1862. In October, he advanced to lieutenant colonel and transferred to the 86th Indiana. His first action with his new unit occurred at Murfreesboro. He was appointed colonel in January 1863 and led the regiment at Chickamauga, Chattanooga and Missionary Ridge. He was wounded during the Atlanta campaign, but he returned to duty in time to fight at Franklin and Nashville. Dick was brevetted brigadier general of volunteers on March 13, 1865.

Dick moved to Bloomington, Illinois, after the war and was appointed postmaster by President Grant. He resigned after twelve years of service to pursue new business opportunities. He died on November 12, 1914, and was buried at Evergreen Memorial Cemetery in Bloomington.

WILLIAM WADE DUDLEY

August 27, 1842–December 15, 1909

William Wade Dudley was born on August 27, 1842, in Weathersfield Blow, Windsor County, Vermont. His father was Reverend John Dudley, a prominent Congregationalist minister and descendant of early Connecticut settlers. After studying at Phillips Academy in Danville, Vermont, and Russell Military Academy in New Haven, Connecticut, he moved to Richmond, Indiana, where he worked as a salesman in an uncle's milling business.

When the Civil War began, Dudley joined a company called the Richmond City Greys and was elected captain. The company was integrated into the 19th Indiana Infantry, which won fame as part of the "Iron Brigade" in the Army of the Potomac. During the first two years of the war, Dudley fought at Second Bull Run, Antietam, Fredericksburg and Chancellorsville. Meanwhile, he was promoted to major and lieutenant colonel. At Gettysburg, he received a severe wound to his right leg, necessitating its amputation. Unfit for field duty, he moved to the Veterans Reserve Corps and served as an army inspector and judge advocate. He was promoted to brevet brigadier general of volunteers on March 13, 1865, for gallantry at Gettysburg.

After the war, Dudley became a lawyer and Republican activist. He was appointed U.S. marshal for Indiana by President Rutherford B. Hayes in 1879 and commissioner of pensions by President James Garfield in 1881. In 1888, he was elected treasurer of the Republican National Committee. During the presidential campaign, he sent a notorious letter to Indiana GOP county chairs encouraging voter fraud. The resulting scandal tipped the election in favor of Democrat Grover Cleveland, who was running against Indiana governor Benjamin Harrison. Dudley died on December 15, 1909, in Washington, D.C., and was buried at Arlington National Cemetery.

WILLIAM McKEE DUNN

December 12, 1814–July 24, 1887

William McKee Dunn was born on December 12, 1814, in Hanover, Jefferson County, Indiana. He attended local public schools, graduated from Indiana University in 1832 and taught for several years at Hanover College. During 1835–36, he attended Yale College. He then studied law, was admitted to the bar in 1839 and practiced in New Albany between 1839 and 1842, when he moved his practice to Madison. A Whig who eventually transitioned to the Republican Party, Dunn served in the Indiana House of Representatives during the 1848–49 session and was a member of the Indiana Constitutional Convention of 1850–51. He was a trustee of Indiana University from 1852 to 1854 and served in the same capacity at Hanover College. In 1856, he was a delegate to the first Republican National Convention and was again elected to the U.S. House of Representatives in 1858.

Dunn remained in the House when the Civil War began, but he also joined the Union army as an aide-de-camp to Major General George McClellan and participated in the Virginia campaign in 1861. Defeated for reelection in 1862, he was promoted to major judge advocate for the Department of Missouri in March 1863 and then advanced to colonel and assistant judge advocate general of the U.S. Army in June 1864. At the end of the war, he was brevetted brigadier general of volunteers to rank from March 13, 1865.

Dunn remained in the Regular Army after the war as lieutenant colonel and assistant judge advocate general until 1875, when he was promoted to brigadier general and judge advocate general. He retired in 1882 and died on July 24, 1887, at Maplewood, his summer residence in Fairfax, Virginia. He was interred at Oak Hill Cemetery in Washington, D.C.

JAMES ADAMS EKIN

August 31, 1819–March 27, 1891

James Adams Ekin was born on August 31, 1819, in Pittsburgh, Pennsylvania. As a youth, Ekin served an apprenticeship as a steamboat builder and then established a successful steamboat construction business. At the outbreak of the Civil War, he enlisted in the 12th Pennsylvania

Infantry as a lieutenant and was appointed regimental quartermaster. He quickly displayed a talent for obtaining needed equipment and supplies and advanced steadily in rank and responsibility with the Quartermaster Department. During 1862 and early 1863, he was a strong presence in Indiana, helping the state to supply its troops and overseeing construction of buildings for the Soldiers' Home and Rest and additional barracks at Camp Morton prison in Indianapolis. He subsequently was promoted to colonel and chief quartermaster of the Cavalry Corps of the Army of the Potomac. He was brevetted brigadier general of volunteers on March 8, 1865; five days later, he received a similar brevet in the Regular Army for meritorious services in the Quartermaster Department.

Ekin remained in the Regular Army after the war, and in 1865, he served on the military tribunal that tried the Lincoln assassination conspirators. In 1866, he was appointed deputy quartermaster general, and in 1872, he was designated commander of the new Western Arsenal in Jeffersonville, Indiana. Designed by Quartermaster General Montgomery Meigs, the magnificent depot supplied vehicles, harness, clothing, heating stoves, cooking ranges, hardware and other items to troops on Reconstruction duty in the South. Colonel Ekin headed the arsenal until his retirement in 1883. Ekin Avenue, which borders the National Cemetery in neighboring New Albany, was named in his honor. Ekin died on March 27, 1891, in Louisville, Kentucky, and is interred at Cave Hill Cemetery.

NEWELL GLEASON

August 11, 1824–July 6, 1886

Newell was Gleason born as Newell Sargeant on August 11, 1824, in Wardsboro, Windham County, Vermont. He changed his surname to Gleason in 1843 and graduated from Norwich University in Vermont in 1849. A civil engineer by profession, he subsequently moved to LaPorte, Indiana. When the Civil War broke out, he joined the 87th Indiana Infantry as a lieutenant colonel in August 1862. He participated with the regiment at Perryville two months later and was promoted to colonel and commander of the 87th in March 1863. During the following months, he led the regiment at Tullahoma, Tennessee, and at Chickamauga in September 1863. Transferred to the XIV Corps, the 87th participated in the storming of

Missionary Ridge in November. Gleason led the regiment through General William T. Sherman's Atlanta campaign during 1864 and later commanded a brigade in the Carolina campaign in 1865. He was brevetted brigadier general of volunteers on March 13, 1865, and was mustered out with his regiment on June 10, 1865.

After the war, Gleason immediately was elected to fill an unexpired term in the state House of Representatives. He also resumed his career in civil engineering, concentrating on railroad bridge construction until his death by suicide on July 6, 1886. His suicide probably stemmed from what is now called posttraumatic stress disorder caused by the violence of the war. He was buried at Pine Lake Cemetery in LaPorte.

OLIVER PAUL GOODING

January 29, 1835–September 19, 1909

Oliver Paul Gooding was born on January 29, 1835, in Moscow, Rush County, Indiana. He graduated from the U.S. Military Academy at West Point in 1858, ranking twenty-fourth in a class of twenty-seven cadets. He was assigned to the 10th U.S. Infantry Regiment as a second lieutenant and served in the Utah Expedition. He was promoted to first lieutenant a month after the Civil War began and was posted in Washington, D.C., until February 1862, when he was commissioned a colonel and appointed commander of the 31st Massachusetts Infantry. The regiment immediately marched south for the New Orleans campaign. From September 1862 to January 1863, Gooding commanded Forts Jackson and St. Philip. He led a brigade in the XIX Corps until July 28, 1863, during operations at Port Hudson, Louisiana. After a leave of absence, he headed the District of Baton Rouge from early September until mid-October 1863 and then served on a military commission in Washington. In January 1864, he returned to Mississippi, where he commanded a brigade from late February through early June and led a division until mid-July during the 1864 Red River campaign. Gooding resigned his volunteer commission in November 1864 and reverted to his Regular Army position with the 10th Infantry as a captain, the rank he had received in June 1862. On March 13, 1865, he was brevetted brigadier general and major general of volunteers for gallant action in the assault on the Confederate works at Port Hudson.

Gooding resigned his Regular Army commission on March 20, 1865. After the war, he moved to St. Louis, where he practiced law, served as city police commissioner and wrote several religious publications based on his wartime experience. He died on September 19, 1909, in Washington, D.C. His body was taken to Greenfield, Hancock County, Indiana, where he was interred at Park Cemetery.

DANIEL F. GRIFFIN

September 20, 1833–February 14, 1865

Daniel F. Griffin was born on September 20, 1833, in the Canadian province of Nova Scotia. His parents moved to Louisville when Daniel was a child, and both died when he was twelve, leaving him an orphan. He was adopted by Thomas McGrain, who took him to his home in Corydon, Indiana. Daniel was educated at Kentucky Military Institute, became a civil engineer and settled in New Albany, Indiana, his wife's hometown. When the Civil War erupted, Griffin joined the 38th Indiana Infantry Regiment, organized by Colonel Benjamin F. Scribner, and was commissioned a lieutenant. The regiment was mustered in on September 18 and posted to General Don Carlos Buell's army at Elizabethtown, Kentucky. During the winter and spring of 1861–62, it patrolled the Green and Nolin Rivers and marched to Bowling Green and Nashville, among other locales in Kentucky and Tennessee. Meanwhile, Griffin advanced to major in March 1862.

In the fall of 1862, the 38th helped repulse Braxton Bragg's invasion of Kentucky and fought at Perryville, where it sustained heavy losses. Over the next two years, Griffin participated in William S. Rosecrans's Tennessee campaign in 1863 and William T. Sherman's Atlanta campaign, the pursuit of John B. Hood and Sherman's March to the Sea in 1864. Meanwhile, Griffin was elevated to lieutenant colonel on September 26, 1863. When Scribner's illness forced his resignation, Griffin took command of the regiment and was promoted to colonel on August 22, 1864. Unfortunately, Griffin contracted typhoid while visiting his wife in New Albany and died there on February 14, 1865. Buried at Fairview Cemetery, he was posthumously brevetted brigadier general of volunteers on March 13, 1865.

CIVIL WAR GENERALS OF INDIANA

IRA GLANTON GROVER

December 26, 1832–May 30, 1876

Ira Glanton Grover was born on December 26, 1832, in Brownsville, Union County, Indiana. After graduating from Indiana Asbury University (now DePauw University) in 1856, he taught school while studying law. He continued to teach after his admission to the bar in 1866. In 1860, he was elected to the Indiana House of Representatives representing Decatur County. He served during the 1861 session but resigned when the Civil War broke out and was appointed a company captain in the 7th Indiana Infantry, a three-month unit. He remained with the regiment when it reenlisted for three years. Grover was wounded at Port Republic on June 9, 1862, but he soon returned to duty and was promoted successively to major in July 1862 and to lieutenant colonel in March 1863. One month later, he advanced to colonel and was given command of the regiment.

At Gettysburg on July 1, 1863, the regiment was assigned to guard corps trains coming into the city on Emmitsburg Road and to await the arrival of a Vermont regiment. When the Vermonters failed to arrive on time, Grover departed for the front in time to reinforce a battered Iron Brigade at Culp's Hill. He later was court-martialed, allegedly for abandoning his post on Emmitsburg Road, but he was exonerated. He was mustered out on September 20, 1864, when the regiment's enlistment expired, and on March 13, 1865, he was brevetted brigadier general of volunteers. After leaving the service, he moved to Greensburg, Indiana, where he practiced law and served as county clerk from 1868 to 1873. He also lost a race for U.S. House of Representatives in 1866. He died in Greensburg on May 30, 1876, and was buried at South Park Cemetery.

BENJAMIN HARRISON

August 20, 1833–March 13, 1901

The only American president elected from Indiana, Benjamin Harrison was born on August 20, 1833, on his family's Ohio River farm in North Bend, Ohio. He was a member of one of the nation's distinguished political dynasties. His great-grandfather Benjamin Harrison signed the

Declaration of Independence and served as governor of Virginia; his grandfather William Henry Harrison was Indiana territorial governor and president of the United States; and his father, John Scott Harrison, served in Congress. Possessed of a powerful intellect and strong Presbyterian religious values, Benjamin graduated from Miami University in 1852, read law in Cincinnati and was admitted to the bar in 1854. Soon thereafter, he moved to Indianapolis and adopted Indiana as his home state. Harrison also entered Republican politics, and in 1860, he was elected reporter of the Indiana Supreme Court.

Harrison remained in office when the Civil War erupted, but when President Abraham Lincoln issued another call for troops in 1862, Harrison offered his services to Governor Oliver P. Morton, who asked him to recruit a regiment. After some hesitation because he lacked military experience, Harrison accepted a commission as colonel and appointed commander of the 70th Indiana Infantry. The regiment entered service in August and was dispatched to Louisville, Kentucky. Over the next two years, the 70th conducted reconnaissance and railroad guard duty in Kentucky and Tennessee and fought in General William T. Sherman's Atlanta campaign. In January 1864, Harrison took command of a brigade and led it at Resaca, Cassville, New Hope Church and Peachtree Creek and during Sherman's March to the Sea.

Although he did not seek the office, Harrison was reelected Supreme Court reporter in October 1864. He returned to Indianapolis, resumed office and launched a lucrative law practice. Over the next decade, he became a rising Republican star. He lost a close gubernatorial race with Democrat James "Blue Jeans" Williams in 1876. But when U.S. Senator Morton died in 1877, Harrison became the state Republican leader, opening his path to election to the U.S. Senate in 1881. Harrison lost for reelection in 1887, but his prominence projected him into the 1888 presidential campaign, in which he ousted President Grover Cleveland. His one term produced much major legislation, including the Sherman Anti-Trust Act, the McKinley Tariff, the Sherman Silver Purchase Act and the Meat Inspection Act. But he failed to overcome Democratic opposition to voting rights protections for African Americans. Defeated by Cleveland in 1892, Harrison resumed his law practice in Indianapolis and accepted several civic positions. He died on March 13, 1901, and was interred at Crown Hill Cemetery.

THOMAS JEFFERSON HARRISON

June 8, 1824–September 28, 1871

Thomas Jefferson Harrison was born on June 8, 1824, in Shelby County, Kentucky. When he was six years old, his family moved to Crawfordsville, Montgomery County, Indiana, where he eventually attended Wabash College. After graduation, he studied law, was admitted to the bar in 1851 and opened a practice in Kokomo. In 1858, he was elected to the Indiana House of Representatives as a Republican. At the outbreak of the Civil War, he joined the 6th Indiana Infantry, a three-month unit, and was commissioned a captain. After participating in General George McClellan's western Virginia campaign, the 6th was reorganized into the 39th Indiana Infantry, a regiment of sharpshooters, with Harrison as colonel and commander. During the next two years, the 39th fought at Shiloh, Stones River, Murfreesboro and Chattanooga. In September 1863, it participated at Chickamauga, after which it was reorganized as the 8th Indiana Cavalry, still under Harrison's command. In 1864, the 8th Cavalry joined General Edward M. McCook's raid against Georgia railroads south of Atlanta and participated in General Hugh Judson Kilpatrick's cavalry raids during Sherman's March to the Sea and the Carolina campaign.

Harrison was mustered out on January 14, 1865, and brevetted brigadier general of volunteers on January 31. He returned to Kokomo but stayed only briefly before moving in 1866 to Tennessee, where he engaged in teaching, farming, journalism and the lumber business. In 1870, he was appointed U.S. marshal for the Middle District. He died in Nashville on September 28, 1871; his body was returned to Kokomo and interred at Crown Point Cemetery.

MORTON CRAIG HUNTER

February 5, 1825–October 25, 1896

Morton Craig Hunter was born on February 5, 1825, in Versailles, Ripley County, Indiana. He followed a preparatory course in the local schools and then studied law at Indiana University in Bloomington. He graduated in 1849 and entered private practice after admission to the bar. He was elected to the Indiana House of Representatives in 1858 and served during the 1859 session. In 1860, he was a delegate to the Republican National Convention that nominated Abraham Lincoln for president of the United States.

Hunter entered Civil War service on November 1, 1861, when he was commissioned a brigadier general in the Indiana Legion, the state militia. He transferred to federal service in August 1862 as colonel and commander of the 82nd Indiana Infantry, which was integrated into the 1st Brigade, 3rd Division, in XIV Corps. At Chickamauga, where Confederate troops under General James Longstreet routed the right wing of the Army of the Cumberland, Hunter took a new position on Horseshoe Ridge and created a line that saved the army from disaster. At Missionary Ridge, Hunter's 82nd Indiana and the 99th Ohio spearheaded the attack on General Braxton Bragg's center, and despite murderous fire, the 82nd was the first Union force to reach the summit. Hunter's gallantry contributed to his appointment as commander of the 1st Brigade, which he led during Sherman's March to the Sea. In January 1866, he was brevetted brigadier general of volunteers, effective March 13, 1865.

After the war, he resumed legal practice. He was elected to Congress in 1866 and served from 1867 to 1869. He was elected again in 1872 and served from 1873 to 1879. He continued his law practice after retiring while also operating a quarry in Indiana's limestone district. He died in Bloomington on October 25, 1896, and was buried at Rose Hill Cemetery.

Gilbert Marquis LaFayette Johnson

November 4, 1837–January 9, 1871

Details of the early life of Gilbert Marquis LaFayette Johnson are obscure. He was born on November 4, 1837, in Cincinnati, Ohio, and at some point, he relocated to Indiana. In September 1861, after the Civil War began, he joined the 2nd Indiana Volunteer Cavalry as a first lieutenant. Organized in Indianapolis and commanded by Colonel John A. Bridgland, the 2nd was the state's first full cavalry regiment. The unit served in Kentucky during the winter of 1861–62. In April 1862, as the regiment rode toward Pittsburgh Landing, Tennessee, with General Don Carlos Buell's Army of the Ohio, Johnson was promoted to captain. After Shiloh, he was appointed assistant inspector general on the staff of Brigadier General James S. Negley.

In March 1864, Johnson was promoted to lieutenant colonel and assigned to the 11th Indiana Volunteer Cavalry. The following month, he was promoted to colonel and given command of the new 13th Indiana Volunteer Cavalry. During 1864, the regiment occupied Huntsville, Alabama. He was mustered out with the regiment on September 25, 1865. In January 1866, President Andrew Johnson nominated Johnson as brevet brigadier general of volunteers to rank from March 13, 1865. After the war, General Johnson returned to Huntsville, where he married the daughter of a prominent citizen and served as postmaster from 1869 until his death on January 9, 1871, the result of injuries sustained during the war. He was buried at Maple Hill Cemetery in Huntsville.

LEWIS JOHNSON

1841–1900

Lewis Johnson was born in Germany in 1841. He spent two years as a cadet in the Prussian navy before immigrating to America. After arriving in New York City, he made his way to Lafayette, Indiana. When the Civil War began, Johnson enlisted in the 10th Indiana Infantry. The regiment deployed to western Virginia, where it and other Indiana regiments secured the mountain counties for the Union. Because of his military training in Germany, Johnson was commissioned a first lieutenant in September 1861 and promoted to captain in August 1862. Meanwhile, the regiment moved west with General William S. Rosecrans and participated in the Battles of Chattanooga, Chickamauga and Missionary Ridge.

In April 1864, after the War Department began recruiting African American troops in the Chattanooga area, Johnson was appointed colonel and commander of the new 44th Colored Infantry Regiment. In October, the 44th was ordered to Fort Hill in Dalton, Georgia, to protect the Western & Atlantic Railroad. On October 13, the fort was attacked by superior forces under General John Bell Hood and forced to surrender. Johnson and his fellow white officers were paroled, but the Black enlisted men were returned to their former masters or impressed as Confederate army laborers. Many of the captives had died by the war's end, but some escaped and rejoined Johnson, who had rebuilt the 44th and, along with new recruits, helped deal Hood a decisive defeat at Nashville. For his leadership, Johnson was brevetted brigadier general, effective March 13, 1865. He was appointed to the Regular Army after the war and continued to command Black troops as captain of the 24th Infantry. Johnson retired from the army in 1898 and died in 1900. The place of his death and location of his burial are unknown.

FIELDER ALSOR JONES

February 27, 1833–January 7, 1882

Fielder Alsor Jones was born on February 27, 1833, in Potter County, Pennsylvania. Little is recorded about his early life. But by the Civil War, he was living in Indiana. When the war erupted, he raised a company and was appointed its captain. It was mustered into the 6th Indiana Volunteer Infantry, a three-month unit commanded by Colonel Thomas T. Crittenden. After the regiment was mustered out, Jones transferred to the new 8th Indiana Cavalry, attached to the 39th Indiana Infantry Regiment, as lieutenant colonel. During his service, Jones and his troops fought at Shiloh, Corinth, Stones River and Murfreesboro and participated in Sherman's Atlanta campaign, the March to the Sea and the Carolinas campaign. Jones was brevetted brigadier general of volunteers, effective March 13, 1865. His postwar life is not recorded. He died on January 7, 1882, in Toledo, Ohio, and was interred at Sharon Center Cemetery, in Sharon Center, Pennsylvania, his hometown.

REUBEN COALBAUGH KISE

August 15, 1840–November 21, 1872

Reuben Coalbaugh Kise was born on August 15, 1840, in Stilesville, Hendricks County, Indiana. His father, William Coalbaugh Kise, served in an Indiana infantry regiment during the Mexican-American War and was a colonel of the 10th and 116th Indiana Infantry Regiments during the Civil War. When the war began, Reuben Kise was living in Lebanon, Indiana. He enlisted in the Union army on April 20, 1861, at age twenty, as a second lieutenant in Company I of the 10ᵗʰ Indiana Infantry, a three-month unit. The regiment mustered out in Indianapolis in August and then reenlisted for three years. In the process, Kise was promoted to first lieutenant.

In June 1862, Kise advanced to captain and was appointed assistant adjutant general to General Mahlon D. Manson. He held that post until March 1864, when he was promoted to major in the new 120ᵗʰ Indiana Infantry, organized at Columbus. Integrated into a brigade of General Alvin P. Hovey's division in the XXIII Corps, the 120ᵗʰ fought in the Atlanta campaign at Resaca and Kennesaw Mountain and the Siege of Atlanta. During the fall, it engaged John Bell Hood's retreating army at Franklin and Nashville. Meanwhile, Kise was promoted to lieutenant colonel in September 1864. After the defeat of Hood, the regiment moved to North Carolina, where it joined General William T. Sherman's army at Goldsboro. For several months after the war ended, the 120ᵗʰ engaged in provost or garrison duty in North Carolina. When commander Allen W. Prather resigned in September 1865, Kise was promoted to colonel and commander. He was brevetted brigadier general in December, effective the previous March. Kise died on November 21, 1872, in Vincennes, Indiana, and was buried at Oak Hill Cemetery in Lebanon.

Frederick Knefler

April 12, 1833–June 14, 1901

Frederick Knefler was born on April 12, 1833, in Arad, Romania, then part of the kingdom of Hungary. During 1848–49, Frederick and his father, Dr. Nathan Knoepfler, a Jewish physician, fought in the Hungarian War for Liberation. When the revolution failed, the family fled to the United States. They landed in New York City and eventually moved to Indianapolis, where they soon became involved in religious and civic life. Frederick studied law, joined a volunteer fire company and became assistant Marion County clerk. He also became acquainted with Lewis Wallace. As civil war neared, he joined a militia company. When war came, Governor Oliver P. Morton appointed Wallace as adjutant general, and Wallace tapped Knefler as his chief assistant. After raising five regiments, Wallace took command of the 11ᵗʰ Indiana Infantry, appointed Knefler a first lieutenant and promoted him to captain in June 1861.

Knefler's relationship with Wallace lasted through the capture of Forts Henry and Donelson and the Battle of Shiloh. After Wallace's removal from field command, Morton made Knefler colonel of the new 79th Indiana Infantry, which he commanded at Stones River, Chickamauga and Missionary Ridge. In 1864, the 79th joined General William Sherman's army for the Atlanta campaign, during which Knefler commanded a brigade. When General John B. Hood invaded Tennessee, Knefler's brigade fought at Franklin and Nashville. After the war, President Andrew Johnson brevetted Knefler a brigadier general of volunteers, effective March 13, 1865. Meanwhile, Knefler returned to Indianapolis, where he opened a law practice, served as head of the pension office and was president of the board of regents of the Indiana Soldiers and Sailors Monument. He died on June 14, 1901, in Indianapolis, and was buried at Crown Hill Cemetery.

William Polke Lasselle

August 17, 1836–January 6, 1896

William Polke Lasselle was born on August 17, 1836, in Indiana, but his precise place of birth is not recorded, nor are the details of his early life. By the beginning of the Civil War, however, he was living in the Logansport area, where he enlisted on April 24, 1861, and was elected a sergeant in Company K of the 9th Indiana Infantry, a three-month unit commanded by Colonel Robert H. Milroy. Three months later, the regiment reenlisted for three years, and Lasselle rejoined his company as captain. During the next two years, the regiment fought at Cheat Mountain, Shiloh, Perryville, Stones River and Chickamauga, before Lasselle was taken prisoner and confined at Macon, Georgia. Meanwhile, he was promoted to major in September 1862 and to lieutenant colonel in April 1863. He was exchanged in September 1864 and subsequently performed duty with his regiment at San Antonio and New Braunfels, Texas, before being mustered out of service on September 28, 1865. He was simultaneously brevetted colonel and brigadier general of volunteers by President Andrew Johnson, effective March 13, 1865. Soon after the war, he relocated to Washington, D.C., where he died on January 6, 1896. He was buried at Oak Hill Cemetery in Washington.

JOHN MARSHALL LINDLEY

April 12, 1831–February 12, 1874

John Marshall Lindley was born on April 12, 1831, in Downington, Chester County, Pennsylvania. There is little record of his early life, but by the Civil War, he was living in Indiana, most likely in the Indianapolis vicinity. When President Abraham Lincoln issued his call for volunteers, Lindley responded by raising a company from his Indianapolis neighborhood. Company F, with Lindley as captain, was mustered into the 19th Indiana Infantry, which was combined with three Wisconsin regiments to create what became the famed Iron Brigade in the Army of the Potomac.

For more than three years, Lindley participated in some of the war's most violent combat. He suffered a leg wound at Brawner's Farm during Second Bull Run but recovered in time for Antietam and Fredericksburg. Promoted to major in May 1863, after the death of his predecessor, he lost a finger at Gettysburg while defending Culp's Hill. With the death of the regiment's commander, Colonel Samuel Williams, at the Wilderness on May 6, 1864, Lindley assumed command and led it at Spotsylvania, Cold Harbor and Petersburg. He was promoted to lieutenant colonel on July 1, 1864. Lindley was mustered out on October 9, 1864, after his heavily battered 19th was combined with two other Hoosier regiments to form the 20th Indiana Infantry. Lindley was brevetted brigadier general of volunteers on March 13, 1865, for gallantry at Gettysburg. He died on February 12, 1874, in Washington, D.C., and was buried at Downington Friends Meetinghouse Cemetery in Downington, Pennsylvania.

DANIEL MACAULEY

September 8, 1836–July 5, 1894

Daniel Macauley was born on September 8, 1836, in New York City. Orphaned at age ten, he learned the bookbinding trade and found employment in Buffalo, where he worked until 1860, when he moved to Indianapolis. At the outbreak of the Civil War, he enlisted in the Indianapolis Zouaves, which became a company in the 11th Indiana Infantry. Less than a month later, he was commissioned a first lieutenant. In May, he moved with the regiment to Evansville to blockade the Ohio River and then deployed to Romney, Virginia, and cleared the town of Confederates. In late August 1861, Macauley was appointed regimental adjutant. The regiment moved west during the following months and fought at Fort Henry, Fort Donelson and Shiloh. Advanced to major in April 1862, he saw action at Corinth, Mississippi, and was promoted to lieutenant colonel in September 1863. In March 1864, he was promoted to colonel and given command of the 11th Indiana. During the spring and summer, the regiment was involved in General U.S. Grant's Vicksburg campaign, and Macauley was wounded at Champion's Hill on May 19.

Macauley resumed command after recovering and conducted operations in Louisiana until July, when the regiment moved to Virginia for Philip Sheridan's Shenandoah Valley campaign. In October, while commanding a brigade at Cedar Creek, Macauley sustained a wound that rendered him unfit for field service. He transferred to the Veteran's Reserve Corps and posted at Baltimore, where he remained until his discharge in July 1865. The same month, he was brevetted brigadier general of volunteers for action at Cedar Creek. He returned to Indianapolis after the war and entered politics as a Democrat. In 1867, he was elected mayor and served until 1873. He died on July 5, 1894, in Managua, Nicaragua; his body was returned to Washington, D.C., for interment at Arlington National Cemetery.

WILLIAM GEORGE MANK

1833–March 21, 1887

William George Mank was born in 1833 in Giessen in the state of Hessen, Germany. At some point, he immigrated to the United States and settled in the Indianapolis area. At the outbreak of the Civil War, he enlisted in Lew Wallace's 11th Indiana Infantry, a three-month unit. When that regiment's enlistment expired, Mank collaborated with another German immigrant, Francis Erdelmeyer, to organize a German company that would become part of the 32nd Indiana Infantry, a predominately German regiment commanded by Colonel August Willich. Mank personally recruited hundreds of men for the regiment.

Mank and the 32nd participated in a succession of engagements, including Rowlett's Station, Shiloh, Corinth and Stones River in 1862; the Tullahoma,

Chickamauga and Chattanooga campaigns in 1863; and Sherman's Atlanta campaign during 1864. Mank himself rose steadily through the ranks. Commissioned a first lieutenant in August 1861, he was promoted successively to captain in May 1862 and major in November 1863. Mustered out of the 32nd Indiana in September 1864, he reentered service as lieutenant colonel of the 8th U.S. Veterans Volunteer Infantry in March 1865. Mank was brevetted brigadier general of volunteers the following December.

Mank fell on hard times after the war. He died in his New York City rooming house on March 21, 1887, and was buried in an unmarked grave in the Lutheran All Faiths Cemetery in the Middle Village neighborhood of Queens. His grave remained unmarked until 1998, when the Sons of Union Veterans of New York City dedicated a headstone in his honor.

Thomas Alexander McNaught

September 8, 1826–March 10, 1919

Thomas Alexander McNaught was born on September 8, 1826, in Spencer, Owen County, Indiana. When the Mexican-American War erupted, he joined a company in the 3rd Indiana Volunteer Infantry as a private and served until July 1847. At the outbreak of the Civil War, he enlisted in the 59th Indiana Infantry, organized at Indianapolis and Gosport and was elected captain after raising a company. Once mustered in, the regiment proceeded to Commerce, Missouri, in February 1862 and reported for duty in General John Pope's Army of the Mississippi. During the next two years, the 59th Indiana fought at the Siege of New Madrid during March 1862; the Siege of Corinth, Mississippi, in May 1862; the Battle of Iuka in September 1862; and General U.S. Grant's Vicksburg campaign, including the Battles of Raymond, Jackson, Champion's Hill and Vicksburg itself. Meanwhile, McNaught rose to major in November 1862. In 1864, McNaught took command of a brigade in the 3rd Division of XV Corps and led it during General William T. Sherman's March to the Sea, from Dalton to Atlanta and the capture of Savannah. He was promoted to lieutenant colonel on April 10, 1865, and to colonel on June 28. McNaught was brevetted brigadier general of volunteers for war service, effective August 4, 1865. He returned to his hometown of Spencer, Indiana, after the war, where he died on March 10, 1919. He was buried at River Hill Cemetery.

JOHN CRAVEN MCQUISTON

August 17, 1823–February 22, 1903

John Craven McQuiston was born on August 17, 1823, in Madison, Jefferson County, Indiana. Still living in southeast Indiana when the Civil War erupted, he volunteered for military service and was appointed a company captain in the 16th Indiana Infantry, then being organized at Richmond, Indiana, by Colonel Pleasant A. Hackleman. The 16th experienced its first combat at Balls Bluff, Virginia, in October 1861. The following spring, the regiment saw action in the Shenandoah. In May 1862, McQuiston was appointed provost marshal for the 4th District of Indiana. He remained in that position until September 1863, when he was promoted to colonel and given command of the new 123rd Indiana Infantry, organized at Greensburg. Assigned to the 2nd Brigade, 1st Division, of the XXIII Corps, Army of the Ohio, the regiment fought in the Atlanta campaign, the Battles of Franklin and Nashville and the Carolinas campaign. When General Joseph E. Johnston surrendered his Confederate army, McQuiston served as a staff officer for the ceremonies. McQuiston was brevetted brigadier general of volunteers on March 13, 1865, and was mustered out at Charlotte, North Carolina, on August 25, 1865. He remained in the South after the war and entered the railroad industry, working variously as an engineer, conductor and roadmaster. He died on February 22, 1903, in Williford, Sharp County, Arkansas, and was buried at Maple Park Cemetery in Springfield, Missouri.

JOHN MEHRINGER

October 12, 1826–October 22, 1906

John Mehringer was born on October 12, 1826, in Germany. His family eventually immigrated to the United States and settled in Indiana. He gained military experience as a member of the army during the Mexican-American War. When the Civil War erupted, he volunteered and was appointed a major in the 27th Indiana Infantry, which was organized in Indianapolis and commanded by Colonel Silas Colgrove. He resigned in January 1862 and later spearheaded organization of the 91st Indiana Infantry. The regiment rendezvoused at Evansville in August 1862, and Mehringer took command as a lieutenant colonel. Attached initially to the District of Kentucky, Department of the Ohio and then to the 1st Brigade, 2nd Division, of the XXIII Corps, the 91st performed garrison duty at numerous posts in Kentucky and Tennessee. Mehringer was promoted to colonel in October 1863, and from June to September 1864, he led the regiment during William T. Sherman's Atlanta campaign, fighting successively at Kennesaw Mountain, Chattahoochee River, Decatur and the Siege of Atlanta. From late September to early November, as commander of the 3rd Brigade, 2nd Division, XXIII Corps, Mehringer participated in operations against John Bell Hood in northern Georgia and northern Alabama and then at Franklin on November 30 and Nashville two weeks later. Mehringer rendered his final service in 1865 when he commanded the division's 2nd Brigade during Sherman's Carolinas campaign. He was brevetted brigadier general to rank from March 13, 1865, and mustered out of the army at Salisbury, North Carolina, in June 1865. He died on October 22, 1906, in Louisville, Kentucky, and was buried at Saint Joseph Catholic Cemetery in Jasper, Indiana.

Abram O. Miller

October 2, 1827–April 25, 1901

Abram O. Miller was born in Ohio on October 2, 1827. After graduating from the University of Louisville in 1856, he settled in Lebanon, Indiana, where he practiced medicine and engaged in banking. When the Civil War began, he helped recruit and was appointed a first lieutenant in the 10th Indiana Infantry, a three-month unit commanded by Colonel Joseph J. Reynolds. After two months, Miller was promoted to captain. The regiment mustered out in August and reenlisted for three years. Miller was again appointed a captain, was immediately promoted to major and advanced to lieutenant colonel in April 1862. During a year of service with the regiment, he saw action at Mill Springs, the Siege of Corinth, Mississippi and Iuka.

Miller was promoted to colonel in August 1862 and given command of the 72nd Indiana Infantry, which was organized at Lafayette and incorporated into fellow Hoosier John T. Wilder's "Lightning Brigade." During 1863, the regiment fought at Murfreesboro, Tullahoma, Chattanooga and Chickamauga, where it sustained heavy losses. In November, the 72nd arrived in Memphis and was attached to General William T. Sherman's army. Beginning in late April, the regiment engaged in a series of battles and skirmishes near Atlanta until the city fell in July. After the capture of Atlanta, the 72nd was ordered to Louisville, where it obtained new horses, and then proceeded to Alabama and joined General James H. Wilson's expedition that captured Selma and Montgomery, Alabama, and Columbus and Macon, Georgia. Miller was brevetted brigadier general of volunteers on March 13, 1865. When the war ended, the 72nd moved to Nashville, where it was mustered out on June 25, 1865. Miller returned to Lebanon after the war and lived there until his death on April 25, 1901. He was buried at Oak Hill Cemetery.

THOMAS JEFFERSON MORGAN

August 17, 1839–July 13, 1902

Thomas Jefferson Morgan was born on August 17, 1839, in Franklin, Johnson County, Indiana. His father was Reverend Lewis Morgan, a founder of Franklin College, the younger Morgan's alma mater. Upon graduation in 1861, Morgan enlisted in the 7th Indiana Cavalry, a three-month unit. When his enlistment expired, he spent a year as a school principal in Atlanta, Illinois. He reentered service as a first lieutenant in the 70th Indiana Infantry on August 1, 1862. Morgan served through the fall of 1863, mostly guarding the Louisville & Nashville Railroad against Rebel raids in Kentucky and Tennessee.

Morgan opposed slavery, and when the War Department began organizing Black units, he recruited and was given command of the 14th U.S. Colored Infantry Regiment at Camp Stanton in Gallatin, Tennessee. He was commissioned lieutenant colonel on November 1, 1863, and promoted to colonel on January 1, 1864. After organizing two more Black regiments, he was put in command of the First Colored Brigade of the Army of the Cumberland and led it through Sherman's Atlanta campaign and the Battle of Nashville. Morgan was brevetted a brigadier general of volunteers on March 13, 1865.

Morgan resigned his commission after the war, attended Rochester Theological Seminary, became a Baptist minister and taught church history at Chicago Theological Seminary. He advocated formation of schools for former slaves and state normal schools to educate teachers. From 1889 to

1893, he served as commissioner of Indian affairs for President Harrison, followed by ten years as secretary of the American Baptist Home Mission Society. He died on July 13, 1902, in Ossining, New York, and was buried at Mount Hope Cemetery in Rochester.

WILLIAM HENRY MORGAN

March 13, 1834–March 3, 1878

William Henry Morgan was born on March 13, 1834, in Piqua, Miami County, Ohio. At some point, he arrived in Crawfordsville, Montgomery County, Indiana, where he attended Wabash College. Upon completing his education, he became a merchant in the city. When the Civil War broke out, he joined the 10th Indiana Volunteer Infantry Regiment, a three-month unit, and was appointed captain and company commander. The regiment immediately joined General George B. McClellan's western Virginia campaign and fought at Rich Mountain. On August 19, he was commissioned lieutenant colonel of the 25th Indiana Infantry, a three-year regiment, which was assigned to General U.S. Grant's army, then operating in Kentucky. Morgan led the regiment at the capture of Fort Donelson in February 1862 and then at Shiloh in April. He was promoted to colonel in May 1862. After Shiloh and through the winter of 1862–63, he commanded the 25th at the Siege of Corinth, Mississippi, and guarded railroads against guerrillas operating in Tennessee and Mississippi. From the spring of 1863 to the end of the year, the regiment performed provost duty at Memphis and exercised scouting duty in Tennessee and Mississippi.

Morgan resigned his commission in May 1864 but returned to service as colonel and commander of the 3rd U.S. Veteran Volunteer Infantry in January 1865. During the next few months, he led the regiment in the Shenandoah Valley in Virginia and at Camp Butler in Springfield, Illinois. Meanwhile, he was brevetted brigadier general of volunteers on March 13, 1865. He was in Kansas City, Missouri, at the time of his death on March 3, 1878, but his body was returned to Crawfordsville and buried at Oak Hill Cemetery.

ANDREW JACKSON NEFF

November 30, 1825–November 26, 1904

Andrew Jackson Neff was born on November 30, 1825, in Preble County, Ohio. His family moved to central Indiana while he was a child. After attending schools in New Castle, Muncie and Winchester, he studied law and was admitted to the bar, entering practice in Hartford City. Neff was elected prosecutor for the 7th Judicial Circuit as a Democrat in 1855. The following year, he was elected to the Indiana House of Representatives representing Blackford County. Reflecting the political turbulence of the day, he switched to the Republican Party in 1858.

In 1862, his service in the legislature having ended, Neff enlisted in the 84th Indiana Infantry, which Colonel Nelson Trusler was organizing in Richmond. He was appointed a first lieutenant and quickly advanced to major. Between late 1862 and 1864, the regiment saw action in Kentucky, Tennessee, Alabama and South Carolina. Meanwhile, Neff was promoted to lieutenant colonel in December 1863. He distinguished himself at Tunnel Hill, Georgia, in February 1864, a factor that contributed to his brevet promotion at brigadier general of volunteers on March 13, 1865.

After the war, he entered journalism and edited the *Winchester Journal* from 1864 to 1869. He returned to the General Assembly, serving in the state Senate in the 1873 and 1875 sessions. He founded the *Putnam County Times* at Greencastle in 1881 and headed it until 1884, when he moved to Tennessee and established the *Maryville Times*. He died on November 26, 1904, in San Antonio, Texas, and was buried at Forest Hill Cemetery in Kansas City, Missouri.

JASPER PACKARD

February 1, 1832–December 13, 1899

Jasper Packard was born in Austintown, Mahoning County, Ohio, on February 1, 1832. He moved with his parents to Marshall County, Indiana, in 1835, where he attended local public schools. He then attended Michigan Central College at Spring Arbor, Oberlin College and University of Michigan, where he graduated in 1855. He settled in La Porte, Indiana, taught school, studied law and was admitted to the bar in 1861.

When the Civil War began, he enlisted as a private in the 48th Indiana Infantry in October 1861. He advanced to first lieutenant on January 1, 1862, and to captain in September 1862. He was wounded during the assault on Vicksburg. In June 1864, he was promoted to colonel and given command of the 128th Indiana Infantry, which he led in the Atlanta campaign, the pursuit of Rebel general John Bell Hood and the Carolinas campaign. He was brevetted brigadier general of volunteers on March 13, 1865, and mustered out in April 1866.

After the war, he resumed a career in journalism, education and Republican politics. He was elected La Porte County auditor in 1866 and served until 1869, when he entered the U.S. House of Representatives. He served three terms and retired in March 1875. He became U.S. Internal Revenue agent the next year and served until 1884. Meanwhile, he published the *La Porte Chronicle* from 1874 to 1878 and the *La Porte Daily Public Spirit* from 1886 to 1888. He moved to New Albany in 1888 and edited the *Evening Tribune* and *Weekly Tribune* for about two years. In 1896, he was elected to the Indiana House of Representatives and served one term, representing Floyd, Clark and Jefferson Counties. In 1899, he was appointed commandant of the State Soldiers' Home in Lafayette, where he died on December 13, 1899, and was interred at the Soldiers' Home Cemetery.

Charles Sherman Parrish

May 25, 1830–September 16, 1907

Charles Sherman Parrish was born on May 25, 1830, in Columbus, Ohio. After attending Ohio Wesleyan University and Kenyon College, he studied law and was admitted to the bar in 1851. The next year, he moved to Decatur County, Indiana, and then to Wabash County in 1854. An adherent of the new Republican Party, he was elected prosecuting attorney for the 11th Judicial Circuit in 1857 and joined a military company called the Wabash Guards the same year.

After the fall of Fort Sumter, Parrish joined the 8th Indiana Infantry and was commissioned a captain. Promoted to major in September, he participated in the Battle of Pea Ridge, Arkansas, in March 1862 and advanced to lieutenant colonel in May 1862. After distinguishing himself in several other battles, he was promoted to colonel and given command of the 130th Indiana Infantry in

March 1864, which had been organized the previous December in Kokomo. Over the next thirteen months, as part of the XXIII Corps, Army of the Ohio, the regiment fought in multiple battles in the Atlanta campaign, the Battles of Franklin and Nashville and the Carolinas campaign. Parrish was brevetted brigadier general of volunteers effective March 13, 1865, and mustered out with his regiment in December 1865.

Parrish resumed his law practice in Wabash after the war. He was elected to the Indiana Senate in 1866 but served only in the 1867 session before resigning to become register in bankruptcy for the U.S. District Court for Indiana. In 1869, he was appointed U.S. inspector of customs in New Orleans and served until 1873, when he returned to Wabash. He was elected mayor in 1878 and served until 1883. He moved to Oklahoma in 1891 and opened a law practice in Cleveland, where he died on September 16, 1907. He was buried at Woodland Cemetery.

MILTON STAPP ROBINSON

April 20, 1832–July 28, 1892

Milton Stapp Robinson was born on April 20, 1832, in Versailles, Ripley County, Indiana. In 1840, his family moved to Decatur County, where he was educated in the local public schools. He studied law, was admitted to the bar in 1851 and moved to Anderson, Madison County, the same year. A Republican in politics, he lost a contest for presidential elector in 1856 and was appointed director of the State Prison North in 1861.

At the start of the Civil War, Robinson joined the 47th Indiana Infantry as a lieutenant colonel. He served with the regiment at the Siege of New Madrid, the capture of Island No. 10 and the Fort Pillow expedition in 1862 before receiving command of the 75th Indiana Infantry in October 1862. Attached to a brigade in XIV Corps in the Army of the Ohio, Robinson led the regiment at Stones River. He subsequently commanded a brigade at Chickamauga in September 1863 and saw further action in Chattanooga, the Atlanta campaign, Sherman's March to the Sea, the Carolina campaign and, finally, the Battle of Bentonville. Robinson was brevetted brigadier general of volunteers, effective March 13, 1865.

Robinson returned to Anderson after the war and served in the Indiana Senate from 1867 to 1870. He was a delegate to the Republican

National Convention in 1872 and served two terms in the U.S. House of Representatives, from 1875 to 1879, succeeding Brevet Brigadier General Morton C. Hunter. He resumed his practice in Anderson after leaving Congress and practiced until 1891, when he was appointed to the Indiana Appellate Court. He subsequently was appointed chief justice and served until his death in Anderson on July 28, 1892. He was interred at Maplewood Cemetery.

Thomas Jackson Rodman

July 31, 1816–June 7, 1871

Thomas Jackson Rodman was born on July 31, 1816, in Salem, Washington, County, Indiana. After an education in the local public schools, he was appointed to the U.S. Military Academy at West Point, where he ranked seventh out of fifty graduates in the class of 1841. In July, Rodman was appointed a brevet second lieutenant in the U.S. Army Ordnance Department, where he would spend his entire career. In 1844, he initiated experiments that changed construction of cast-iron cannon by eliminating constraints that prevented the manufacture of larger, more powerful weapons. Rodman saw limited action in the Mexican-American War and was promoted to first lieutenant in March 1847. Most of the next decade, he was stationed at the Fort Pitt Foundry in Pittsburgh, where he was promoted to captain in 1855 and developed the fifteen-inch, smoothbore columbiad cannon, for which the War Department approved production in 1859. These so-called Rodman Guns were the nation's main coastal defense weapons through the rest of the nineteenth century.

During the Civil War, Rodman commanded the Watertown Arsenal in Watertown, Massachusetts. Promoted to major in June 1863, he concentrated on designing the twenty-inch cannon. Because of his specialty, Rodman never attained the field command that normally would earn a general's commission. But on March 13, 1865, he received brevet promotions to lieutenant colonel, colonel and brigadier general. He remained in the Regular Army after the war, but before moving to his next command, he endured a politically motivated Congressional investigation of his management of the Watertown Arsenal. After being cleared, he took command of Rock Island Arsenal in Illinois, where he died on June 7, 1871. He was buried at the Rock Island National Cemetery.

CHARLES SAWYER RUSSELL

March 15, 1831–November 2, 1866

Charles Sawyer Russell was born on March 15, 1831, in Boston, Massachusetts, where his father was a publisher and seed dealer. In 1855, he married an Indianapolis woman and relocated to her hometown. When the Civil War broke out, Russell enlisted in the Union army as a sergeant and was promoted quickly to captain in the 11th U.S. Infantry Regiment and stationed at Fort Independence in Boston. He was brevetted a major for his service at Antietam and brevetted lieutenant colonel for his gallantry at Chancellorsville. Russell mustered out of the 11th Infantry, and on May 1, he was promoted to full lieutenant colonel and assigned to organize and command the 28th Colored Infantry Regiment. Formed at Camp Fremont in Indianapolis, it was the only Black unit formed in Indiana.

Upon completion of its training, the 28th left Indianapolis for Petersburg, Virginia, where it lost half of its force in the disastrous Battle of the Crater in July. On July 30, Russell was simultaneously brevetted colonel and brigadier general of volunteers. He was advanced to the full rank of colonel on August 27 and was given command of a brigade in the IX Corps of the Army of the Potomac. He held that command until October, when he transferred to the Army of the James and led a succession of brigades in the XXV Corps from December 3 to February 27, 1865. When Richmond fell in early April, Russell had the honor of leading the 28th into the city. The regiment was mustered out on November 8, 1865, in Texas and returned to Indianapolis for a public reception. Russell took command of the 20th U.S. Infantry in September 1866 and moved it to Cincinnati, where he died during a cholera epidemic that hit the city and the regiment two months later. He was buried at Spring Grove Cemetery in Cincinnati.

BENJAMIN FRANKLIN SCRIBNER

September 20, 1825–November 29, 1900

Benjamin Franklin Scribner was born on September 20, 1825, in New Albany, Floyd County, Indiana. He was the son of Abner Scribner, one of the city's founding brothers. Possessed of a military bent, he joined a militia group called the Spencer Greys. When the Mexican-American War erupted in 1846, the Greys joined the 2nd Indiana Infantry. Scribner saw action at Buena Vista and was promoted to sergeant before being mustered out a year later. After his discharge in 1847, he published a war memoir entitled *Camp Life of a Volunteer*.

In civilian life, Scribner was a chemist and druggist, and he ran the partnership of Scribner & Maginness, a large drug firm, with Edmund A. Maginness. When the Civil War began, Scribner and fellow Floyd Countian William W. Tuley organized a company that became part of the Indiana Legion, the state militia. Both were appointed colonels. In September 1861, Scribner was made colonel for the 38th Indiana Infantry, a three-year regiment organized at New Albany. During the next two years, Scribner led the regiment at Stones River, Chickamauga, Lookout Mountain and Kennesaw Mountain. Scribner resigned because of ill health in August 1864, after being brevetted brigadier general of volunteers.

In 1865, Scribner obtained a position as collector of Internal Revenue for the Second Indiana District, a post he held until 1871. He then rejoined the drug business, which Maginness had operated in his absence. Upon his return, Scribner opened a short-lived branch in New York City. He left the business in 1878 when he was appointed treasury agent in Alaska. His length of service is not clear. Scribner was active in veterans affairs and published *How Soldiers Were Made; or the War as I Saw It Under Buell, Rosecrans, Thomas, Grant and Sherman* in 1887. He died in Louisville, Kentucky, on November 29, 1900, and was buried at Cave Hill Cemetery.

JOHN PETER CLEAVER SHANKS

June 17, 1826–January 23, 1901

John P.C. Shanks was born on June 17, 1826, in Martinsburg, Virginia (now West Virginia), where he began his education. In 1839, he moved to Jay County, Indiana, where he completed his formal education and studied law. He was admitted to the bar in 1848 and began practicing in Portland. During the next decade, he also worked as a farmer, teacher, publisher and hotelier. A Whig who became a Republican, he served brief stints as Jay County auditor and prosecutor. In 1854, he was elected to the Indiana House of Representatives and served one term. After a few years out of office, he was elected to the U.S. House of Representatives in 1860 and served from 1861 to 1863, losing in a Democratic wave.

Despite his legislative position, when the Civil War began, he joined the Union army as a colonel and aide-de-camp to General John C. Frémont. He served in that capacity from September 20 to November 19, 1861, and again from March 31, 1862, to October 9, 1863. He then took command of the 7th Indiana Cavalry and fought in several cavalry engagements, including the pursuit of Sterling Price in Arkansas and Missouri in 1863 and multiple raids by General Benjamin Grierson in Mississippi between late 1863 and 1865. On March 13, 1865, he was brevetted brigadier general of volunteers. He was mustered out of the army on September 19, 1865.

After the war, Shanks was reelected to Congress and served from March 1867 to March 18, 1875. Defeated for renomination in 1874, he resumed his law practice and was again elected to the Indiana House of Representatives in 1879. He died in Portland on January 23, 1901, and was buried at Green Park Cemetery.

DAVID SHUNK

September 23, 1822–February 21, 1865

David Shunk was born on September 23, 1822, in Taneytown, Carroll County, Maryland. He served as a captain in the Mexican-American War and was a carriage maker in Indiana at the outbreak of the Civil War. He enlisted in the 8th Indiana Infantry in April 1861 and was immediately commissioned a captain. One week later, he advanced to major. Before the regiment's three-month enlistment expired, it fought at the Battle of Rich Mountain in western Virginia. In September 1861, when the regiment reenlisted for three years, Shunk was promoted to lieutenant colonel. In March 1862, Shunk led the regiment at the Battle of Pea Ridge in Arkansas, and he was promoted to colonel two months later. During the next fifteen months, the 8th fought at Port Gibson, Jackson, Champion's Hill and Black River Ridge. When the leaders of the 33rd Illinois Infantry were incapacitated at Vicksburg, Shunk assumed its command along with his own. During the Shenandoah Valley campaign in 1864, Shunk led the 8th Indiana at Opequon, Fisher's Hill and Cedar Creek. On February 9, 1865, he was brevetted brigadier general of volunteers for his leadership at Vicksburg. Mustered out the same day because of a virus, he returned home to Marion, Grant County, Indiana, where he died on February 21, 1865. He was interred at Estates of Serenity Cemetery in Marion.

JOHN SMITH SIMONSON

June 2, 1796–December 5, 1881

By far the eldest of all Indiana Civil War generals, John Smith Simonson was born on June 2, 1796, in Uniontown, Pennsylvania. He received a public school education and attended Washington and Jefferson College in Washington, Pennsylvania. After service as a captain in the Indiana Militia during the War of 1812, he settled in Charlestown, Indiana, then the Clark County seat, where he became a farmer, miller and merchant. He also studied law and was admitted to the bar in 1833. A Jacksonian Democrat, he served as county sheriff from 1822 to 1826 and justice of the peace from 1829 to 1833. Between 1826 and 1829, he served in the Indiana Senate, representing Clark and Floyd Counties. Simonson resumed military duty in 1832 as a captain in the Black Hawk War and retained close military ties. In 1840, he was elected to the Indiana House of Representatives and served through 1846, becoming Speaker of the House during his final term.

The end of Simonson's legislative term coincided with the outbreak of the Mexican-American War. President James K. Polk asked him to raise a company of mounted riflemen, which he led as captain. Brevetted major for gallantry at Chapultepec, he remained in the service and was promoted to major in 1853 and colonel in 1861, when he retired at age sixty-five. His retirement was brief. In November, Governor Oliver Morton appointed him superintendent of the Volunteer Regiment Service as chief mustering and disbursing officer. In September 1863, the War Department designated Simonson commander of the District of Indiana, a position he held until May 1864. Brevetted brigadier general of volunteers on March 13, 1865, he served as post commander of Indianapolis during 1866–67, when he settled claims of deceased soldiers. Civically, he was a Freemason and president of the Clark County Historical Society in 1876. He died on December 5, 1881, in New Albany and was buried at the Charlestown Cemetery.

WILLIAM THOMAS SPICELY

January 25, 1823–February 15, 1884

William Thomas Spicely was born on January 25, 1823, in North Carolina. His family migrated to Orange County, Indiana, and settled in Orleans. When the Mexican-American War began, he enlisted and won a battlefield commission as captain for gallantry at Buena Vista. Spicely's experience in Mexico made him a prime candidate for military leadership when the Civil War erupted. When Colonel Cyrus M. Allen began organizing the 24th Indiana Infantry Regiment in Vincennes in June 1861, Spicely volunteered and was commissioned a captain. The unit was mustered in on July 31 and placed under command of Colonel Alvin P. Hovey. Spicely was promoted to major on April 5, 1862, and the regiment experienced its first major combat at Shiloh the following two days. On April 29, during the Siege of Corinth, Mississippi, Spicely advanced to lieutenant colonel, and on May 14, he rose to colonel. Later in the summer, he succeeded to regimental command after Hovey advanced to brigade command.

In 1863, Spicely commanded the regiment during General U.S. Grant's Vicksburg campaign, fighting at Port Gibson and Champion's Hill and the siege of the city. He subsequently advanced to brigade command, and in the spring of 1865, his brigade fought in the Mobile campaign, including the Battle of Fort Blakely from April 2 to April 9. Spicely was brevetted a brigadier general of volunteers on March 26, 1865, for his leadership in the Siege of Mobile. He was mustered out on November 15, 1865; he died in New Albany, Indiana, on February 15, 1884, and was buried at Green Hill Cemetery in Orleans.

BENJAMIN JOHN SPOONER

October 27, 1823–April 8, 1881

Benjamin John Spooner was born on October 27, 1823, in Mansfield, Ohio. By the time of the Mexican-American War, he was living in the Ohio River town of Lawrenceburg, Indiana. When the war erupted, he volunteered for the 3rd Indiana Infantry Regiment and was commissioned a second lieutenant. Meanwhile, he studied law and opened an office in Lawrenceburg after the war.

When the Civil War began, Spooner joined the 7th Indiana Infantry, a three-month unit, and was commissioned a captain on April 18, 1861. Because of his prior military experience, he was promoted to lieutenant colonel just nine days later. After fighting at Philippi in George McClellan's western Virginia campaign, the 7th was mustered out, and Spooner joined the 51st Indiana as lieutenant colonel in December 1861. He led the regiment at Shiloh and Corinth before resigning in June 1862. In November 1862, he was commissioned colonel and given command of the 83rd Indiana Infantry. It fought at Vicksburg, Missionary Ridge and the Atlanta campaign, and Spooner lost his left arm at Kennesaw Mountain. During the fall of 1864 he served on the military commissions that tried the treason cases of Lambdin P. Milligan, Harrison H. Dodd, Dr. William Bowles and other leaders of the Sons of Liberty, which spearheaded pro-Confederate opposition to the war in Indiana. Because of his wartime performance, Spooner was brevetted both brigadier general and major general of volunteers on March 13, 1865. He resigned his commission in May 1865. Shortly thereafter, he was appointed U.S. marshal for the District of Indiana and served until 1879. He died on April 8, 1881, in Lawrenceburg and was buried at Greendale Cemetery.

ISRAEL NEWTON STILES

July 16, 1833–January 17, 1895

Israel Newton Stiles was born on July 16, 1833, in Suffield, Hartford County, Connecticut. Educated in the public schools, he moved to Lafayette, Indiana, in 1852. There he studied law and was admitted to the bar in 1854. A Republican in politics, he served as Tippecanoe County prosecutor from 1856 to 1858, when he was elected to the Indiana House of Representatives representing Tippecanoe County. He also was active in the antislavery movement and delivered more than sixty speeches during John C. Frémont's 1856 presidential campaign.

When the Civil War began, Stiles enlisted as a private in the 20th Indiana Infantry. In July, he was appointed adjutant with the rank of first lieutenant. In September, he saw action at Hatteras Inlet, North Carolina, and was captured at Malvern Hill, Virginia, in May 1862. Released from Libby Prison in Richmond six weeks later, he immediately advanced to major in the new 63rd Indiana Infantry, which was assigned to guard railroads in Kentucky. Promoted to lieutenant colonel in the summer of 1863 and to colonel in March 1864, Stiles commanded the regiment at Rocky Face Ridge, Snake Creek Gap and Resaca during General William T. Sherman's Atlanta campaign and at Franklin and Nashville in December 1864. He was brevetted brigadier general of volunteers on January 31, 1865, and in February led his regiment to Raleigh, North Carolina, for garrison duty. Stiles was mustered out in Indianapolis in June 1865.

After the war, Stiles relocated to Chicago, where he developed a successful law practice and served for four years as city attorney. He died in Chicago on January 17, 1895, and was buried at Pine Ridge Cemetery in the village of Loda, Iroquois County, Illinois.

ABEL DELOS STREIGHT

June 17, 1828–May 27, 1892

Abel Delos Streight was born on June 17, 1828, in Wheeler, Steuben County, New York. Although his education was limited, he was ambitious and had a talent for carpentry that led him into the lumber-milling industry. He started his first mill at age nineteen and opened another soon after. In 1858, he moved into lumber sales, first at Cincinnati and then at Indianapolis, where he acquired an interest in the Indianapolis Chair Company.

At the onset of the Civil War, Streight volunteered and was commissioned lieutenant colonel in the 51st Indiana Infantry. He fought at Shiloh, Perryville and Stones River. He gained notoriety in April 1863 by leading a two-thousand-man raid from Nashville into northern Alabama. His objective was to destroy Southern railroads. But the enterprise was fraught with problems, including that many of the troops rode mules rather than horses. The raid also was harassed by General Nathan B. Forrest's Confederate cavalry, and on May 3, Forrest's troops captured Streight and his command near Rome, Georgia. Streight was detained at Libby Prison in Richmond, Virginia, until February 9, 1864, when he was one of more than one hundred officers who escaped and one of fifty-nine who eluded recapture. After an extended rest, he returned to duty as commander of the 1st Brigade, 3rd Division, IV Corps, and participated in the Battles of Franklin and Nashville. Streight was brevetted brigadier general of volunteers effective March 13, 1865, and resigned from the Army on March 16.

Streight returned to Indianapolis after the war and resumed the lumber business. A Republican, he was elected to the Indiana Senate in 1876 and made an unsuccessful bid for the 1880 gubernatorial nomination. He died on May 27, 1892, and was buried at Crown Hill Cemetery.

DeWitt Clinton Thomas

March 21, 1828–May 9, 1882

DeWitt Clinton Thomas was born on March 21, 1828, in Salem, Washington County, Indiana, which remained his lifelong home, except during his military service. When the Civil War began, he joined the 18th Indiana Infantry, organized in Indianapolis and was appointed a major on August 16, 1861. He fought at Pea Ridge, Arkansas, in March 1862 and then transferred to the new 93rd Indiana Infantry, organized at Madison, as its commander with the rank of colonel. Mustered into service in October 1862, the regiment participated in noncombat operations in Tennessee, Mississippi and Arkansas during the ensuing fall and winter. During the spring, the regiment was ordered to Duckport, Louisiana, where it joined the XV Corps for General U.S. Grant's Vicksburg campaign, in which its service included combat at the Siege (and capture) of Jackson and the Siege of Vicksburg.

In June 1864 the 93rd fought at Brice Crossroads, Mississippi. A series of minor engagements followed in Tennessee, Arkansas, Missouri and Kansas before the regiment returned to Tennessee for the Battle of Nashville in December. After little more than a month in winter quarters, Thomas took the regiment to Dauphin Island, Alabama, where it took position for the Siege of Spanish Fort, followed by the assault on Fort Blakely. After periods of occupation duty at Montgomery, Selma and Gainesville, Alabama, the regiment was mustered out at Memphis on August 10, 1865. Thomas was brevetted brigadier general of volunteers, effective March 13, 1865. He returned to Salem and lived there until his death on May 9, 1882. He was interred at Crown Hill Cemetery in Salem.

JACOB GARETSON VAIL

1827–October 9, 1884

Jacob Garetson Vail was born in 1827. Neither the precise date nor location of his birth is recorded, but most probably he was born in Gibson County, Indiana. The details of his early life are equally obscure. By 1860, however, Vail had become a prominent figure in Gibson County. When President Abraham Lincoln issued his first call for troops, Vail helped spearhead the recruitment of a company from the Princeton area and was commissioned its captain. The company was assigned to the 17th Indiana Infantry as mounted infantry. Vail led the company through several major engagements, including Chickamauga and Chattanooga, before his promotion to major in April 1864. In August, he was promoted to lieutenant colonel of the 17th Mounted Infantry and engaged in a succession of cavalry operations after succeeding John T. Wilder as regimental commander. He was promoted to colonel in November 1864 and brevetted brigadier general of volunteers on March 13, 1865.

Vail returned to Gibson County after the war and engaged in politics as a Republican. Except for a few months in 1868, he was Gibson County sheriff from 1866 to 1870 and again from 1876 to 1878. He later moved to Leavenworth, Kansas, where he died on October 9, 1884, and was buried at Mount Muncie Cemetery in Lansing, Kansas.

HENRY DANA WASHBURN

March 28, 1832–January 26, 1871

Henry Dana Washburn was born on March 28, 1832, in Woodstock, Vermont. After studying in the common schools, he became a tanner, currier and schoolteacher. He moved to Vermillion County, Indiana, in 1850 and then attended the New York State and National Law School. He graduated in 1853, passed the bar and opened a practice in Newport, Indiana. He soon entered politics and was elected Vermillion County auditor in 1854, serving until 1861.

After the Civil War began, Washburn joined the Union army on August 16, 1861, and was appointed lieutenant colonel of the 18th Indiana Infantry.

He fought at Pea Ridge in March 1862 and was promoted to colonel and given command of the regiment in July. In 1863, the 18th Indiana joined the XIII Corps in General U.S. Grant's army for the Vicksburg campaign, fighting at Port Gibson, Champion's Hill and in the Siege of Vicksburg, during which Washburn led a brigade. After Vicksburg fell, he led the brigade in the capture of several Confederate forts in Louisiana. In January 1864, he took his troops to Virginia, where they saw heavy action at Opequon, Fisher's Hill and Cedar Creek. On December 15, 1864, Washburn was brevetted brigadier general of volunteers. In the spring, his brigade participated in raids against Rebel forces in the Savannah, Georgia area. Upon nomination by President Andrew Johnson, Washburn was brevetted major general of volunteers, effective March 13, 1865.

After the war, Washburn resumed law practice and was elected to two terms in the U.S. House of Representatives. In 1869, he was appointed surveyor general of Montana and served until his death. In 1870, he led the Washburn-Langford-Doane expedition that explored the future Yellowstone Park, where Mount Washburn is named for him. He died on January 26, 1871, at his home in Clinton, Indiana, where he was buried at Riverside Cemetery.

FRANK WHITE

Frank White is perhaps the least documented and most obscure of all Indiana Civil War generals of any type. He apparently was born in Ohio, but we have no record of the precise date or location of his birth. Likewise, little is known of his early life, except that by the Civil War he was living in Greencastle, Putnam County. Also, he is often confused with Brevet Brigadier General Frank White, who hailed from New York.

When the war began, Indiana's Frank White joined the 15th Indiana Infantry as a captain and company commander. The regiment was mustered in on June 12, 1861, and saw action during the next few months in western Virginia, including the Battle of Rich Mountain. In November 1861, the regiment joined General Don Carlos Buell's army in Louisville and later fought at Shiloh, Corinth and Perryville. In late 1862, the 15th Indiana was integrated into General William S. Rosecrans's Army of the Cumberland and fought the following months at Stones River, Tullahoma and Chattanooga. In March 1863, White was promoted to major. Two months later, he advanced to lieutenant colonel and transferred to the 17th Indiana Infantry, commanded by Colonel John T. Wilder. During 1864, the 17th participated in Sherman's March to the Sea, and late in the war, White commanded a brigade in 2nd Division of the Cavalry Corps of the Military District of Mississippi. He was brevetted brigadier general of volunteers effective March 13, 1865. The details of White's postwar career, death and burial are not recorded.

JOHN THOMAS WILDER

January 31, 1830–October 20, 1917

John Thomas Wilder was born on January 31, 1830, in Hunter, Green County New York. He descended from a line of soldiers who had fought in the Revolutionary War and the War of 1812. In 1849, after an education in the local schools, Wilder headed out on his own, settling first in Columbus, Ohio, where he worked as a draftsman and millwright, experience that would become the foundation of his career. In 1857, he relocated to Greensburg, Indiana, where he operated a small foundry, produced hydraulic machines, built mills and sold equipment.

When the Civil War began, Wilder organized a light artillery company, and his foundry cast two six-pound cannons. When the federal government declined his service, the company joined the 17th Indiana Infantry, with Wilder as captain. In July, the regiment left for western Virginia with the cannons in tow. The company was reorganized as the 26th Battery, Light Artillery. Wilder was commissioned lieutenant colonel in June and promoted to colonel and regimental commander in March 1862. In September, he had to surrender his garrison at Munfordville, Kentucky, to General Simon B. Buckner's superior force. Exchanged in November, Wilder resumed command and mounted his regiment and three others on horses to create the "Lightning Brigade." Armed with repeating rifles, Wilder's Brigade executed many mobile maneuvers during the Tullahoma, Chattanooga and Atlanta campaigns. Brevetted brigadier general of volunteers in August 1864, he resigned for health reasons in October and returned home.

After the war, Wilder moved to East Tennessee, where he engaged in iron manufacturing and other enterprises. He was elected mayor of

Chattanooga in 1871 and later served as postmaster, federal pension agent and commissioner of the Chickamauga and Chattanooga National Military Park. He died on October 20, 1917, while vacationing in Jacksonville, Florida. He was buried at Forest Hills Cemetery in Chattanooga.

REUBEN WILLIAMS

August 15, 1831–January 15, 1905

Reuben Williams was born on August 15, 1831, in Tiffin, Seneca County, Ohio. By the Civil War, he had relocated to Indiana, possibly Kosciusko County. When the war began, he enlisted and was commissioned a second lieutenant in Company I of the 12th Indiana Infantry, a one-year regiment organized in Indianapolis and commanded by Colonel James M. Wallace. In August, before the regiment departed for the East, Williams was promoted to captain. During its initial year, the regiment saw duty at Harpers Ferry, Virginia, and Williamsport and Sharpsburg, Maryland. In early March 1862, it skirmished near Winchester, Virginia, and subsequently saw action in the Shenandoah Valley. Mustered out after a year of service, the 12th Indiana reenlisted for three years on August 17, 1862. Colonel William H. Link took command of the reorganized regiment, with Williams second-in-command as lieutenant colonel.

Attached to Charles Cruft's brigade in the Army of the Kentucky, the 12th Indiana fought at Richmond on September 20. Link was killed in battle, and Williams took command. He was promoted to colonel two months later. He led the regiment through the rest of the war and participated in a succession of major engagements, including the Siege of Vicksburg, the Chattanooga campaign, Missionary Ridge, the Atlanta campaign, Sherman's March to the Sea, the Carolinas campaign and, finally, the Battle of Bentonville. Meanwhile, during late 1864, Williams served on the military commissions that conducted the Sons of Liberty treason trials in Indianapolis. Williams was brevetted brigadier general of volunteers, effective March 13, 1865.

After the war, Williams resided in Warsaw, Indiana, where he established the *Northern Indianan*, forerunner of today's *Warsaw Times-Union*. He died in Warsaw on January 15, 1905, and was interred at Oakwood Cemetery.

EDWARD H. WOLFE

September 26, 1834–August 17, 1916

Edward H. Wolfe was born on September 26, 1834, in Rushville, Indiana. Educated at Miami University in Oxford, Ohio, and Hanover College, he was a merchant before the Civil War. When the war began, he joined the 52nd Indiana Infantry, a three-year regiment organized by Colonel James M. Smith at Rushville and Indianapolis. Wolfe was immediately appointed a major. The regiment was attached to a brigade in the Army of the Tennessee, and it first saw action at Fort Henry and Fort Donelson in February 1862. In June, after combat at Shiloh and Corinth, Colonel Smith resigned his commission, and Wolfe, who had been promoted to lieutenant colonel in April, took command and was promoted to colonel in September.

Under Wolfe's command, the 52nd Indiana performed garrison duty at various posts, including Fort Pillow, in Tennessee, engaged guerrillas in Tennessee and Arkansas in late 1862 and January 1864 and participated in the expedition against Jackson, Mississippi, in September 1863. The regiment fought in the Red River campaign during the spring of 1864 and engaged at various encounters in Louisiana, Mississippi, Arkansas, Tennessee and Missouri before fighting at Nashville in December.

After the war, President Andrew Johnson nominated Wolfe as brevet brigadier general of volunteers, effective March 13, 1865. Meanwhile, Wolfe returned to Rushville, entered politics and was elected Indiana auditor as a Republican in 1880; he served from January 1881 to January 1883, succeeding General Mahlon D. Manson. Wolfe died at Rushville on August 17, 1916, and was buried at East Hill Cemetery.

JOHN WOOLLEY

1824–April 6, 1873

John Woolley (also spelled Wooley) was born in New York City in 1824. The details of his early life are sketchy, but by the Civil War, he was a banker and living in Indiana. When President Abraham Lincoln called for volunteers, Woolley joined the 2nd Indiana Cavalry as its adjutant with the rank of first lieutenant on October 3, 1861. A short time later, he transferred to the 5th

Indiana Cavalry and was promoted to major in March 1862. In June 1862, he transferred briefly to the 4th Michigan Cavalry, with a similar position, before moving back to the 2nd Indiana Cavalry on June 11. Woolley remained with the 2nd Cavalry until March 1863, when he was assigned to the newly organized 5th Indiana Cavalry. Promoted to lieutenant colonel on March 8, 1864, he was appointed four days later to provost marshal for General Lew Wallace in Baltimore. Woolley remained in that position through January 1866. Meanwhile, he was nominated brevet brigadier general of volunteers by President Andrew Johnson to date from March 13, 1865.

After leaving the service in January 1866, he was a partner for several years in a claim collection and real estate agency. In 1870, he became deputy governor of the National Home for Disabled Volunteer Soldiers in Milwaukee, Wisconsin. He held that post until 1872. He died on April 6, 1873, in Milwaukee and was buried at Wood National Cemetery.

STATE SERVICE GENERALS

JAMES E. BLYTHE

November 8, 1819–July 4, 1864

James E. Blythe was born on November 8, 1819, in Lexington, Kentucky. He attended Hanover College near Madison, Indiana, graduating in about 1838. He then moved to New Jersey and studied law while teaching at Woodbury Academy. Admitted to the bar in 1840, he returned to Indiana and settled in Evansville, where he practiced law and engaged in politics. Initially a Whig, Blythe served in the Indiana House of Representatives in 1847 but lost a race for presidential elector in 1848. He was a delegate to the Constitutional Convention of 1850–51, which drafted the state's present constitution. He subsequently aligned with the nativist American or Know-Nothing Party during the 1850s and was reelected to the state House of Representatives for the 1859 term. He supported the Constitutional Union Party in the 1860 presidential election.

When the Civil War erupted, Blythe was instrumental in organizing the 2nd Regiment, 1st Brigade, of the Indiana Legion, the state militia. The 1st Brigade consisted of companies from Vanderburgh and ten surrounding counties. The brigade was commanded first by Brigadier General Andrew Lewis, with Blythe as colonel. When Lewis took a new command in the fall, Blythe assumed command and was commissioned brigadier general by Governor Oliver P. Morton on November 1, 1861. During Blythe's three years of leadership, the 1st Brigade was instrumental in guarding Indiana's southern boundary against incursions by Kentucky guerrillas in the Evansville area, particularly during Colonel Adam "Stovepipe" Johnson's raid on Newburgh in September 1862. In July 1863, Blythe's brigade helped protect Camp Morton, the prisoner of war camp in Indianapolis, against General John Hunt Morgan's raiders. Blythe remained in command until his death on July 4, 1864. He was interred at Oak Hill Cemetery in Evansville.

ALEXANDER CUMMINS DOWNEY

September 10, 1817–March 26, 1898

Alexander Cummins Downey was born on September 10, 1817, in Cincinnati, Ohio. His family moved in 1818 to what is now Ohio County, Indiana, where he lived most of his life. He was educated in a log schoolhouse and the county seminary in Wilmington, then the Dearborn County seat. He subsequently worked as a farmer, carpenter, cooper, cabinetmaker and flatboat builder. After reading law with Wilmington lawyer J.T. Brown, he was admitted to the bar in 1841 and entered practice with his mentor. In 1844, he moved to Rising Sun, seat of the new Ohio County, and in 1850, he was appointed judge of the 3rd Circuit Court. Soon after, he was elected by the General Assembly to the same seat under the constitution of 1816. In 1852, after adoption of the new constitution, he was elected judge of the new 1st Circuit, which absorbed the former 3rd Circuit. He organized and taught at the Asbury University Law School, served as its dean after his term on the court and served on the university's board of trustees.

When the Civil War began, Downey enlisted as a private in the Indiana Legion. His prominence resulted in his appointment by Governor Oliver P. Morton as brigadier general of the 4th Brigade, 1st Division, on November 1, 1861. Under his leadership, elements of the brigade participated in the pursuit of General John Hunt Morgan's raiders in July 1863, including the defense of the Jennings County Courthouse in Vernon. Downey was elected to the Indiana Senate in 1862 as a War Democrat and served until 1866. In 1870, he was elected to a six-year term on the Indiana Supreme Court. He returned to the trial bench in 1891, becoming the only jurist in Indiana history to serve as a circuit judge under both constitutions and on a trial bench both before and after sitting on the Supreme Court. He died of a stroke on March 26, 1898.

JAMES HUGHES

November 24, 1823–October 21, 1873

James Hughes was born on November 24, 1823, in Baltimore, Maryland, where he was educated in the common schools. He moved to Monroe County, Indiana, in 1837 and attended Indiana University. He subsequently received an appointment to the U.S. Military Academy, but he dropped out before graduating. He studied law and was admitted to the bar in 1842. When the Mexican-American War began, he volunteered and served as a lieutenant. In 1852, he was elected judge of the 6th Circuit Court and served until 1856, when he was elected to the U.S. House of Representatives, serving one term. Meanwhile, he taught law at Indiana University from 1853 to 1856. In 1859, he was appointed to the U.S. Court of Claims and served until 1864.

Despite his judicial position, Hughes's military experience brought him into the war effort. On July 1, 1863, Governor Morton commissioned him brigadier general and commander of the 2nd Brigade, 2nd Division, of the Indiana Legion. The ink on his commission had barely dried when he and the brigade were called to help resist John Hunt Morgan's raid through southern Indiana. When intelligence indicated that New Albany and Jeffersonville were safe, he took his troops to Mitchell and gathered two thousand more to defend that area or any other threatened locale. When Morgan swung toward Jennings County, Hughes quickly transported his force by rail toward Vernon, forcing the raiders to make a quick exit. In August 1864, Hughes was promoted to major general and given command of the 2nd Military Division. In that capacity, he joined General Alvin P. Hovey to thwart Colonel Adam "Stovepipe" Johnson's raid on Newburgh, Indiana. He resumed his law career after the war, served as the cotton agent for the U.S. Treasury Department and represented the Italian and Spanish embassies in Washington. He died on October 21, 1873, in Bladensburg, Maryland.

HENRY JORDAN

September 11, 1835–May 1906

Henry Jordan was born on September 11, 1835, in Corydon, Indiana. His father was Colonel Lewis Jordan, who commanded the Home Guard at the Battle of Corydon. He attended Corydon Seminary and pursued higher education at Indiana University and Miami University in Oxford, Ohio. He was elected to the Indiana House of Representatives from Harrison County in 1858, served one term and lost a race for the Indiana Senate in 1860. For the first three years of the war, Jordan served in the 17th Indiana Mounted Infantry, reaching the rank of lieutenant colonel. On August 9, 1864, Governor Oliver P. Morton commissioned Jordan brigadier general of the 1st Brigade, 2nd Division, of the Indiana Legion. He succeeded Brigadier General James Hughes, who had been promoted to major general and command of the division. For several months, he focused most of his effort on guarding the Ohio River border between New Albany and Troy. But Jordan's primary service appears to have been to investigate a conspiracy by disloyal elements in Crawford and Orange Counties to foment draft resistance and aid Confederate guerrillas from Kentucky engaged in robberies. His investigations elicited confessions by, and arrests of, numerous men affiliated with the Sons of Liberty and Knights of the Golden Circle.

After the war, Jordan practiced law, farmed and edited the *Corydon Republican.* He also served as U.S. deputy collector of Internal Revenue and register in bankruptcy for the U.S. District Court in Indianapolis from 1877 to 1881. He subsequently moved to Greencastle, Indiana, where he died in May 1906.

ANDREW LEWIS

April 19, 1813–March 10, 1877

Andrew Lewis was born on April 19, 1813, in Lewisberry, Pennsylvania. He showed an early affinity for medicine, and after completing his studies, he left his hometown in 1835 and established a medical practice in Princeton, Gibson County, Indiana. His practice flourished and gave him a public profile that carried him into civic affairs, including promotion of the Evansville & Crawfordsville Railroad and drainage improvements to the Wabash River bottoms during the 1850s. When the Civil War started, he adhered to the Union and played a leading role in recruiting troops for the army. On June 7, 1861, Governor Oliver P. Morton commissioned him brigadier general of the 1st Brigade, 2nd Division, of the Indiana Legion. He remained in the post just a few months before resigning to help recruit volunteer regiments for the Union army. In October 1861, he organized the 58th Indiana Infantry at Princeton and was appointed its colonel. Shortly thereafter, he resigned and proceeded to recruit the 65th Indiana Infantry, also at Princeton, and served temporarily as its colonel. After the war, he continued to promote transportation and other civic improvements in Princeton and Gibson County. He died in Princeton on March 10, 1877, and was buried at Maple Hill Cemetery.

JOHN LOVE

January 9, 1820–January 29, 1881

John Love was born on January 9, 1820, in Culpepper County, Virginia. He moved to Tennessee as a youth and was appointed to the U.S. Military Academy at West Point. He ranked fourteenth among the fifty members of the class of 1841 and was appointed a brevet second lieutenant in the 1st Dragoons. He was commissioned a full second lieutenant in February 1842 and spent the next four years at Carlisle, Pennsylvania, and various western assignments, including an expedition with General Stephen Kearney. Love was promoted to first lieutenant in 1846 and served with Kearney during the Mexican-American War, commanding an artillery battalion at Santa Cruz Rosales, Mexico. After postwar service at several western posts, he resigned in 1853 and settled with his wife in Indianapolis. For the next eight years, he dealt in real estate, operated a farm and built railroads. In 1858, he joined the Indiana Legion as a captain.

When the Civil War began, Love served as major and chief of staff to Brigadier General Thomas A. Morris of the Indiana Volunteers. In July 1861, the brigade participated in the western Virginia campaign, fighting at Laurel Hill, Rich Mountain and Corrick's Ford. Love mustered out upon coming home and was given command of a volunteer training camp in Indianapolis. On September 10, 1861, Governor Oliver P. Morton appointed him major general of the Indiana Legion. In July 1862, he helped repel Adam Johnson's raid on Newburgh. He resigned on January 1, 1863, but was recalled to head resistance to John Hunt Morgan's raid in July 1863. Love mobilized a large brigade and forced Morgan to withdraw early from Vernon. He then resumed his real estate business and represented the Gatling Gun Company to several foreign nations. In 1880, Congress appointed him manager of the National Home for Disabled Volunteer Soldiers. He died on January 29, 1881, in Indianapolis and was interred at Crown Hill Cemetery.

JOHN LUTZ MANSFIELD

January 6, 1803–September 20, 1876

Born Johann B. Lutz on January 6, 1803, in Braunschweig, Germany, Mansfield was educated at universities in Gottingen and Heidelberg, before immigrating to the United States in 1824. He soon settled in Lexington, Kentucky, where he served as professor of mathematics and civil engineering at Transylvania University and briefly as acting president on two occasions in the 1830s. About 1858, he relocated to Jefferson County, Indiana. A Republican in politics, he was elected to the Indiana House of Representatives in 1858 and served one term; he was a presidential elector in 1860.

When the Civil War began, Governor Oliver P. Morton appointed Mansfield brigadier general of the 3rd Brigade, 1st Division, of the Indiana Legion on September 10, 1861. In August 1862, during the Confederate invasion of Kentucky, his brigade was mobilized to defend the state's Kentucky border and to guard Camp Morton in Indianapolis. In October 1862, Mansfield also served simultaneously for eight days as colonel of the 54th Indiana Infantry. In July 1864, he was promoted to major general of the 1st Military Division, comprising five brigades, and served until November 1865. Meanwhile, Mansfield was elected to the Indiana Senate in 1862 and served in the 1863 session.

In 1870, Mansfield moved to Piatt County, Illinois, and settled in a small village that was later named in his honor on March 3, 1876. During retirement, he was active in the Grand Army of the Republic. He died on September 20, 1876, and was buried at the Mansfield Cemetery.

ISAIAH MANSUR

April 14, 1824–December 3, 1880

Isaiah Mansur was born on April 14, 1824, on a farm in Salsburg, Wayne County, Indiana. In 1825, his parents moved from their farm to Richmond, where his father conducted a general merchandise business until 1847, when the family moved to Indianapolis. Mansur received his early education in the Richmond public schools and then moved on to Miami University in Oxford, Ohio, where his roommate was future governor Oliver P. Morton. Their friendship lasted until Morton's death. After leaving Miami, Mansur returned to Indianapolis, where he worked for a year in a pork-packing plant owned by his father and brother. He then studied law with Judge John S. Newman, who also was Morton's mentor. As Mansur was completing his studies, his father's health failed, and he found it necessary to join the pork-packing company. During the next several years, he helped build it into one of the city's leading industrial enterprises.

On April 15, 1861, just days after the Civil War began, Governor Morton tapped his Miami classmate to serve as commissary general, with the responsibility for acquiring and distributing food and related supplies for the thousands of troops flooding into Indianapolis in response to President Abraham Lincoln's call for volunteers. Mansur strove to provide the best provisions and made significant personal financial contributions. But the rapid influx of supplies and reports of poor management in the distribution of commodities triggered a legislative investigation that prompted Mansur's resignation on May 27, 1861. He resumed his business interests, and in 1863, he was instrumental in establishing the Citizens National Bank. In his later years, he was involved in many benevolent endeavors. He died at his home in Indianapolis on December 3, 1880, and was buried at Crown Hill Cemetery.

THOMAS ARMSTRONG MORRIS

December 26, 1811–April 1, 1904

Thomas Armstrong Morris was born on December 26, 1811, in Nicholas County, Kentucky. His family moved to Indianapolis in its pioneer years, and his father served as Indiana auditor. After attending the local schools,

Thomas became a printer's apprentice with Indiana's first newspaper. In 1830, after additional studies, he was appointed to West Point, where he graduated fourth in the class of 1834. Assigned to the 1st U.S. Artillery, he served tours at Fort Monroe in Virginia and Fort King in Florida. He later held several engineering posts, including one in Indiana, where he helped extend the National Road to Illinois. While in Indiana, he left the army to become the state resident engineer. In that post, he oversaw construction of the Central Canal and the Madison & Indianapolis Railroad. He later served as president of both the Bee Line and Indianapolis & Cincinnati Railroads. He also joined the Indiana Militia as a colonel.

When the Civil War erupted, Governor Oliver P. Morton appointed Morris quartermaster general with responsibility to equip state troops. On April 27, 1861, he was commissioned brigadier general in the state militia. In July, Morris led a brigade of state troops into western Virginia, where he functioned as Union commander at Philippi, Rich Mountain and Corrick's Ford. After the campaign, Morris resumed his duties as quartermaster general. In October 1862, Morris was offered commissions as brigadier general and major general of volunteers. But he declined both offers and resigned his state commission, soon thereafter to return to the railroad business. In 1877, he was appointed to the commission that oversaw construction of the new state capitol building. He also supervised construction of Union Station between 1886 and 1888 and later served as president of the Indianapolis Water Company. He died on April 1, 1904, in Indianapolis and was buried at Crown Hill Cemetery.

JOHN CHALFANT NEW

July 6, 1831–June 4, 1906

John Chalfant New was born on July 6, 1831, in Vernon, Jennings County, Indiana. After a public school education, he attended Bethany College in Bethany, Virginia (now West Virginia), and graduated in 1851. He then studied law, was admitted to the bar in 1852 and opened a law office in Indianapolis. A Republican in politics, he was appointed Marion County deputy clerk in 1853 and served until 1856, when he was elected county clerk. Upon the expiration of his term in 1861, he was elected to fill a vacant seat in the Indiana Senate and served during the 1863 session. Meanwhile, on May 30, 1862, thirteen months after the beginning of the Civil War, Governor Oliver P. Morton commissioned him to succeed John H. Vajen Jr. as quartermaster general. He served until October 13, 1862, during which he worked with Captain James A. Ekin of the U.S. Quartermaster General Department to supply uniforms and equipment to troops organized in the state. He also initiated construction of barracks at various locations throughout the state to house troops being organized into regiments.

Upon his resignation, New resumed his legal practice and expanded into banking and publishing. In 1865, he became cashier of the First National Bank of Indianapolis and served for a decade. In 1875, President Ulysses S. Grant appointed him U.S. treasurer, and he served through the following year. In 1880, New and his son bought the *Indianapolis Journal* and its printing company, and the senior New became the publisher. He served as state Republican chairman in 1880 and 1882. New returned to the Treasury Department as first assistant secretary during 1882–83 and was U.S. consul general in London from 1889 to 1893. He died on June 4, 1906, in Indianapolis and was buried at Crown Hill Cemetery.

ASAHEL STONE

June 29, 1817–February 25, 1891

Asahel Stone was born on June 29, 1817, in Washington County, Ohio. He was educated in Cincinnati, came to Indiana in 1839 and settled in Winchester, Randolph County. At various times, he was a farmer, banker, nurseryman and building contractor who built railroads, turnpikes and other internal improvements. A Whig who transitioned to the Republican Party in the 1850s, Stone was elected to the Indiana House of Representatives in 1846 and served one term. He was elected to the Indiana Senate in 1860 and served during the 1861 special session.

In late May 1861, after the Civil War began, Governor Oliver P. Morton commissioned Senator Stone to replace the beleaguered Isaiah Mansur as commissary general. At that point, Stone resigned his Senate seat. During the next eighteen months, Stone initiated changes that improved both the quality of food and the efficiency of its distribution. A significant factor in his success was his frequent visits to regiments in the field, which gave him a sense of soldiers' wants and needs. Stone remained commissary general until October 1862, when he replaced John C. New as quartermaster general. Stone acquitted himself equally effectively in that post, executing responsibilities that ranged broadly, including supplying uniforms, arms and other equipment to Indiana Legion troops; providing rations and other goods to soldiers on furlough at the Soldiers' Home and Rest; and overseeing the State Bakery. Stone remained quartermaster general until March 1867, when all accounts were settled.

Stone held a variety of business and civic posts after the war, including president of the Randolph County Bank and secretary-treasurer and general manager of the Winchester Wagon Works. He also returned to the state House of Representatives for the 1871 term. He died on February 25, 1891, and was buried at Fountain Park Cemetery in Winchester.

WILLIAM HENRY HARRISON TERRELL

November 13, 1827–May 16, 1884

William Henry Harrison Terrell was born on November 13, 1827, in Henry County, Kentucky. In 1828, his family moved to Bartholomew County, Indiana. He had limited formal education, but he was intellectually curious and gained a liberal education through reading and self-instruction. He joined the Madison & Indianapolis Railroad in 1846 as a clerk in Edinburgh. He soon entered journalism as editor and publisher of the *Columbus Gazette*, a staunch Whig organ. In 1852, Terrell was elected Bartholomew County recorder. While in office, he read law and was admitted to the bar. When his term expired, he opened a legal practice in Vincennes, where he quickly earned a reputation as a man able to get things done in many areas.

Terrell's reputation came to the attention of Governor Oliver P. Morton, and when the Civil War erupted, the governor appointed him military secretary. As such, Terrell compiled lists of Indiana companies in service, their location and information about where they might see future action. He later became Morton's finance secretary and was charged to administer the nearly $1 million that Morton had borrowed from private individuals to fund state war costs. Terrell was finance secretary until November 1864, when Morton appointed him adjutant general with the rank of colonel. In March 1865, through an act of the General Assembly, Morton promoted him to brigadier general, with pay and other allowances equal to those for comparable rank in the Regular Army. Terrell served as adjutant general until May 1869, when he resigned to accept appointment by President U.S. Grant as third assistant postmaster general. In 1873, he became U.S. pension agent in Indianapolis. He retired in 1877 and returned to private business. He died in Indianapolis on May 16, 1884, and was buried at Crown Hill Cemetery.

RICHARD WIGGINTON THOMPSON

June 9, 1809–February 9, 1900

Richard Wigginton Thompson was born on June 9, 1809, in Culpeper County, Virginia. After education at an Episcopal school, he studied law and in 1831 moved to Lawrence County, Indiana, where he was admitted to the bar in 1834. Meanwhile, Thompson joined the Indiana Militia as a second lieutenant in 1832. He was promoted to captain in 1833 and appointed military aide to Governor Noah Noble in about 1834 with the honorary rank of colonel. Thompson was elected to the Indiana House of Representatives as a Whig in 1833 and served until 1836, when he moved to the state Senate and served in the 1836–37 session. He was a presidential elector in 1840 and was elected to the U.S. House of Representatives for the 1841–43 term. He moved to Terre Haute in 1843, served as city attorney in 1846–47 and then returned to Congress for the 1847–49 session. He attended the Whig National Convention in 1852, but he became increasingly nativist during the 1850s and chaired the Know-Nothing state convention in 1856. In 1860, he adhered to the Constitutional Union Party, serving as a delegate to both the state and national conventions but subsequently gravitated to the Republican Party.

In November 1861, Governor Oliver P. Morton commissioned him brigadier general and commander of the 6th Brigade of the Indiana Legion. He served until May 1863, when he entered national service as captain and provost marshal of the 7th Congressional District.

Thompson returned to politics after the war and served in several judicial and administrative posts, including judge of the 18th Indiana Circuit in 1867 and U.S. secretary of the navy from 1877 to 1880. He also served on the boards of Indiana State Normal School at Terre Haute, Indiana Asbury University and Rose Polytechnic Institute. He died on February 9, 1900, and was buried at Highland Lawn Cemetery in Terre Haute.

JOHN HENRY VAJEN JR.

March 19, 1828–May 28, 1917

John Henry Vajen Jr. was born on March 19, 1828, in Hanover, Germany, where his father was a university professor. The family immigrated to the United States in 1836, making stops in Baltimore and Cincinnati before settling in 1839 near Seymour in Jackson County, Indiana. There, his father, now a Lutheran minister, established the largest log church in Indiana. After his father's death in 1845, Vajen moved to Cincinnati and clerked in a large hardware store. Three years later, he bought a financial interest in the firm. Vajen left the business in 1851 and moved to Indianapolis, where he established what became a very successful hardware company.

In late April 1861, Governor Oliver P. Morton asked Vajen to serve as quartermaster general when Thomas A. Morris resigned to accept command of the Indiana Legion. Vajen hesitantly accepted, and for good reason. The task was overwhelming, and military officers and civilian employees alike were unfamiliar with the forms and procedures involved in procuring, storing and distributing military equipment and other goods. Nevertheless, Vajen brought a high degree of order to the process and managed to equip regiments in a timely manner. He remained at his post until March 17, 1862, when he resigned and returned to his private business. In 1864, he was instrumental in organizing the banking house of Fletcher, Vajen & Company, which merged into Fourth National Bank in 1865 and later into Citizens National Bank, for which he was a large stockholder and director. He also engaged in real estate development and reentered the hardware business. Vajen remained a prominent business and civic presence in Indianapolis until his death on May 28, 1917. He was buried at Crown Hill Cemetery.

BIBLIOGRAPHY

A Biographical History of Eminent and Self-Made Men of the State of Indiana. 2 vols. Cincinnati, OH: American Biographical Publishing Company, 1875.

Boatner, Mark M., III. *The Civil War Dictionary.* New York: David McKay Company Inc., 1959.

Charlestown Community History. Charlestown, IN: Clark's Grant Historical Society, 1989.

Coddington, Edwin B. *The Gettysburg Campaign: A Study in Command.* New York: Charles Scribner's Sons, 1968.

Conway, W. Fred. *Corydon: The Forgotten Battle of the Civil War.* New Albany, IN: FBH Publishers, 1991.

Cox, Jacob D. *Sherman's March to the Sea: Hood's Tennessee Campaign and the Carolina Campaigns of 1865.* New York: DaCapo Press, 1994.

Dictionary of American Biography. 20 vols. New York: Charles Scribner's Sons for the American Council of Learned Societies, 1928–35.

Dunn, Jacob Piatt. *Greater Indianapolis: The History, the Industries, the Institutions, and the People of a City of Homes.* 2 vols. Chicago: Lewis Publishing Company, 1910.

———. *Indiana and Indianians: A History of Aboriginal and Territorial Indiana and the Century of Statehood.* 5 vols. Chicago and New York: American Historical Society, 1919.

Eicher, John, and David J. Eicher. *Civil War High Commands.* Palo Alto, CA: Stanford University Press, 2002.

Faust, Patricia L., ed. *Historical Times Illustrated Encyclopedia of the Civil War.* New York: Harper and Row, Publishers, 1986.

Fuller, A. James. *Oliver P. Morton and the Politics of the Civil War and Reconstruction.* Kent, OH: Kent State University Press, 2017.

Gaff, Alan D. *On Many a Bloody Field: Four Years in the Iron Brigade.* Bloomington: Indiana University Press, 1992.

Glatthaar, Joseph. *Forged in Battle: The Civil War Alliance of Black Soldiers and White Officers.* New York: Free Press, 1990.

Gugin, Linda C., and James E. St. Clair, eds. *The Governors of Indiana.* Indianapolis: Indiana Historical Society Press and Indiana Historical Bureau, 2006.

———. *Indiana's 200: The People Who Shaped the Hoosier State, 1816–2016.* Indianapolis: Indiana Historical Society Press, 2015.

———. *Justices of the Indiana Supreme Court.* Indianapolis: Indiana Historical Society Press, 2010.

Horwitz, Lester V. *The Longest Raid of the Civil War: Little-Known and Untold Stories of Morgan's Raid into Kentucky, Indiana, and Ohio.* Cincinnati, OH: Farmcourt Publishing Inc., 1999.

Hughes, Nathaniel Cheairs, Jr., and Gordon D. Whitney. *Jefferson Davis in Blue: The Life of Sherman's Relentless Warrior.* Baton Rouge: Louisiana State University Press, 2002.

McDowell, Robert E. *City of Conflict: Louisville in the Civil War.* Louisville, KY: Louisville Civil War Roundtable, 1962.

Rockenbach, Stephen L. *War Upon Our Border: Two Ohio Valley Communities Navigate the Civil War.* Charlottesville: University of Virginia Press, 2016.

Shepherd, Rebecca, Charles W. Calhoun, Elizabeth Shanahan-Shoemaker and Alan F. January, eds. *A Biographical Directory of the Indiana General Assembly.* Vol. 1, *1816–1899.* Indianapolis: Indiana General Assembly and Indiana Historical Bureau, 1980.

Terrell, William H.H. *Indiana in the War of the Rebellion: Report of the Adjutant General.* Indianapolis: Indiana Historical Bureau, 1960.

Thornbrough, Emma Lou. *Indiana in the Civil War Era, 1850–1880.* Indianapolis: Indiana Historical Bureau and Indiana Historical Society, 1965.

Warner, Ezra J. *Generals in Blue: Lives of the Union Commanders.* Baton Rouge: Louisiana State University Press, 1964.

———. *Generals in Gray: Lives of the Confederate Commanders.* Baton Rouge: Louisiana State University Press, 1959.

ABOUT THE AUTHOR

D r. Carl E. Kramer is founder and vice-president of Kramer Associates Inc., a public history consulting firm based in Jeffersonville, Indiana. He is the retired director of the Institute for Local and Oral History and adjunct assistant professor of history at Indiana University Southeast, where he taught for thirty-five years, including a course on Civil War and Reconstruction. Dr. Kramer is the author of thirteen other books, including *This Place We Call Home: A History of Clark County, Indiana* (Indiana University Press, 2007); *Capital on the Kentucky: A 200-Year History of Frankfort and Franklin County*; and *Rivers of Time: A History of American Commercial Lines, 1905–2015.* He also has authored numerous book chapters and articles published in peer-reviewed academic journals, trade publications and popular magazines. Other publications include nearly three dozen articles in various historical reference works and more than fifty book reviews and review essays.

Dr. Kramer has served on the board of directors of the Urban History Association, on the Publications Advisory Boards of the *Register of the Kentucky Historical Society* and the *Filson Historical Quarterly* and on award juries for the Urban History Association, the Society for American City and Regional Planning History, the Filson Historical Society and the Kentucky Historical Society. He is the former historian of the Indiana Planning Association and currently serves on the board of commissioners of the Jeffersonville Housing Authority, the boards of directors of the Clark County Museum and the Louisville Historical League and on the Indiana Lewis and Clark Expedition

Commission. Dr. Kramer's degrees include a BA cum laude in history and political science from Anderson University, an MA in urban education from Roosevelt University, an MS in community development from the University of Louisville and a PhD in American history from the University of Toledo. His professional honors include the Indiana Historical Society's Dorothy Riker Hoosier Historian Award in 2012, the Louisville Historical League's Founders Award for 2018 and the Captain Donald T. Wright Award for Maritime Journalism, presented in 2019 by the Herman T. Pott National Inland Waterways Library in St. Louis. That award honored Kramer's book *Rivers of Time*. He was honored in 2013 as a Sagamore of the Wabash, Indiana's highest civilian award, by Governor Michael Pence.